Essential

Exercises

for

Training Horses

Essential Exercises

for

Training Horses

An Illustrated Guide

by Sally O'Connor

Half Halt Press, Inc.
Boonsboro, Maryland

ESSENTIAL EXERCISES FOR TRAINING HORSES
An Illustrated Guide

Published 2006 in the United States of America by
Half Halt Press, Inc.
P.O. Box 67
Boonsboro, MD 21713
www.halfhaltpress.com

The Editors thank Diann Landau for her assistance with the
illustrations in this book.

Photos © Leslie Clift

Printed in China

Library of Congress Cataloging-in-Publication Data

O'Connor, Sally.
  Essential exercises for training horses : an illustrated guide / by
Sally O'Connor.
      p. cm.
  Includes index.
  ISBN 0-939481-73-1
  1. Horses--Training. 2. Horses--Exercise. I. Title.
  SF287.O26 2006
  636.1'0835--dc22

                                                    2006021353

To all the horses in my life, past, present and future.

Table of Contents

Just a Horse

From time to time, people tell me, "Lighten up, it's just a horse,"
or, "That's a lot of money for just a horse."
They don't understand the distance traveled, the time spent or
the costs involved for
"just a horse."

Some of my proudest moments have come about with
"just a horse."

Many hours have passed when my only companion was
"just a horse."
But I did not once feel slighted.

Some of my saddest moments have been brought about by
"just a horse."

In those days of darkness, the gentle touch of
"just a horse"
gave me comfort and reason to overcome the day.

If you think it's "just a horse," then you probably understand
phrases like "just a friend," "just a sunrise," or "just a promise."

"Just a horse"
brings into my life the very essence of friendship, trust, and pure
unbridled joy.

"Just a horse"
brings out the compassion and patience that make me a better
person.

Because of
"just a horse"
I will rise early, work hard, and look longingly to the future.

So for me and folks like me, it's not
"just a horse,"
but an embodiment of all the

hopes and dreams of the future...

the fond memories of the past...

and the pure joy of the moment.

"Just a horse"
brings out what's good in me and diverts my thoughts away from
myself and the worries of the day.

I hope that someday they can understand it's not
"just a horse,"
but the thing that gives me humanity
...and keeps me from being....
"just a person."

Anonymous

Acknowledgements

This book was made possible only with the help of many people who contributed much effort and encouragement

I owe a tremendous debt to my teachers over the years who patiently taught me the basics of horsemanship and a deep respect for horses themselves, always stressing the fact that the horses must be comfortable in their work.

I must also thank my own students who talked me into writing down all the exercises I make them do in clinics.

I am eternally grateful to Jacqueline Badger Mars for her generous support over the years to the O'Connor family, and especially for giving me the opportunity to work with Ringmoylen, the little horse featured throughout the book. The beautiful facilities at her home, Stonehall Farm in The Plains, Virginia made a fitting background for most of the pictures. Sue Clarke, the barn manager, and the staff at Stonehall, went above and beyond the call of duty. Leslie Clift provided the excellent photographs taken both at the farm and in competitions as the horse's education progressed. And Jen Racey was the perfect groom, always turning the horse out in immaculate fashion both at home for schooling and providing her loyal support at the shows.

Beth Carnes of Half Halt Press as usual contributed her unfailing support and guidance; I am fortunate to have a publisher who believes.

Introduction

If you spend your lifetime training horses you find that you never stop learning. Each horse is an individual and presents a different challenge. While the basic principles apply to all horses, a readiness to adapt your training methods for a particular animal is the key to being a successful trainer.

I am still learning after years spent training many horses. Good horsemanship is universal. When you go to clinics or observe other riders working their horses you can add to your repertoire. We can learn from other disciplines in addition to the traditional dressage training.

When I give clinics I try to use exercises that will produce results for riders to take home and practice by themselves. Some of these exercises are quite specific and will only be useful to solve temporary problems. These can be discarded once they have worked to good effect. Some of the exercises are used in the progression of training and lead to more sophisticated exercises as the horse develops strength and balance. Others are useful at any time during the training process.

Show ring tests are all based on traditional school figures. However, when you are training, you will find yourself doing movements and using different combinations and techniques you won't find in any dressage test but produce great results.

I have been fortunate to work with some great trainers and have learned from them as well as from studying their writings. You cannot learn to train a horse from books, you need practical riding experience, but you can glean many helpful hints if you supplement your riding with reading.

This book is not about the type of horse to choose, nor what tack you should use, but about exercises I have found useful with many horses and with many students over the years. The difficulty with putting these exercises into a book is that I keep adding new ones along the way. Many of the exercises included here are not in my previous book, **Common Sense Dressage**, because I had not discovered them at the time. However, some exercises in that book are carried over into this one because they are timeless.

1

Flexions,
In Hand and Under Saddle

I have to admit at the beginning of this chapter that I had a debate with myself about including the unmounted flexions in a book for general use. While flexions have been part of traditional dressage training for many years, they are no longer universally used because, if overdone, they can create more difficulty than they cure. So if you want to try these you need to be aware of the pitfalls and to use the exercises with great discretion. Not all horses need to be worked this way, but to overcome stiffness and rigidity of the neck and jaw, these exercises can be valuable tools.

The head and neck are most important influences on the horse's balance. Watch horses play in the open field and you will see them use the neck and head as a counter balance when galloping around turns. The horse has a great range of movement in the neck and this is a big factor in creating the proper connection between the hindquarters and the forehand. A good trainer will stretch and supple the neck and jaw muscles to relax them, thus creating communication and acceptance of the bridle.

Flexions are used at the onset of training, to help the horse find his balance. Once the horse has understood you do not need to repeat these lessons, they can be discarded. Flexions can be used to good effect to overcome resistance of the jaw and to teach the horse to accept an elastic contact.

Flexions of the Jaw

Before you work your horse mounted you can work on the flexion of the jaw while on foot. Stand beside your horse just in front of the shoulder. Take the left rein in your right hand and the right rein in the left hand with your hands just behind the jaw. Gently draw your hands in opposite directions putting pressure on the lower jaw. Maintain the pressure until the horse relaxes his jaw or slightly opens his mouth. Once the horse yields, immediately release the pressure and praise the horse. You must remember that horses do not really understand what is required and you must show them physically. And the best reward is to give the moment the horse gives. This carries on throughout your entire training. Give the horse a chance to understand each new demand.

If your horse leans heavily on your hand and does not seem to realize it must yield the jaw, stand in front of the horse and exert pressure by taking one rein backwards towards the horse the other one forward towards you. Once you have achieved your goal return to the former exercise.

Do not overdo these exercises. Repeat the exercise several times but don't belabor the point. Short sessions often repeated are preferable to a long drawn out struggle. Be content with the little progress at a time and the horse has more of a chance to stay relaxed and not develop mental and physical tension. A relaxed horse will learn, a tense horse will only develop more resistance.

Flexions of the Neck

As soon as the horse understands how to yield his jaw, the next exercise is to teach him to flex and relax his neck. Again, begin by standing on the left side of your horse. Bring the right rein over the base of the neck and hold the left rein about four inches from the bit. Ask the horse to yield his jaw. When he yields, increase the pull on the right rein to turn the head to the right. As you do this, raise your left hand towards the ears to prevent the head from tipping or ducking behind the pressure. The poll

should remain the highest point of the neck. Once you can do this on the left, bending the head to the right, change over to the other side and do the same exercise to obtain a left bend.

Direct Flexion

To teach your horse to give at the poll and in the jaw, you next work on the direct flexion of the poll. Stand by the horse's shoulder, holding the right rein over the neck, and use the left rein to ask for a flexion. You control the height of the mouth by raising or lowering your left hand. By exerting pressure on the reins, you ask the horse to yield. Again, immediately relax the pressure when the horse gives any indication of yielding.

Words of warning: do not let the horse duck below the pressure, and the horse must not avoid the issue

by overbending the neck or leaning on the bit. The purpose of this exercise is to teach the horse to relax the jaw and allow the impulsion to reach your hand once you are mounted and going forward.

Stretching the Neck

By stretching the neck you allow the horse to relax. To teach your horse to stretch, stand beside the head and cross the reins beneath the horse's jaw. Exert a downward pressure evenly on both reins. Be content with any indication of the horse lowering his neck.

Eventually you want to be able to get the horse's head down close to the ground, but remember, the horse must understand the concept before you can achieve this. Your horse must be in a submissive state to trust you enough to lower his head. A tense horse carries his head high looking for his enemies; in order to lower the head, he must develop complete trust.

Stand in front of your horse and press down with both reins until he drops his head and neck.

Once the horse understands, you can get him to lower his head with just a slight pressure on one rein.

Some horses give in quickly; some are much harder to convince. Take the time to have the horse understand the question you are asking.

When your horse can put his head close to the ground, walk him forward for a couple of steps without allowing him to raise his head. You then know the horse is submissive.

With this exercise, you are showing the horse "the way to the ground". A horse that has learned this lesson will be able to perform the "stretchy" circles in trot and canter found in some of the modern dressage tests. Once a horse has learned this concept you can reward him during your training sessions by allowing him to stretch down and out. This loosens the neck and back and improves the strides.

As a judge, I all too often see people throw the reins at the horse in the hope he will somehow stretch down. Often the result is just the opposite: the head goes upward, making me want to comment "The horse should stretch down, not up!" A horse that accepts the contact and that is "on the bit" will follow the rider's hand and stretch down when allowed to do so.

Flexions while Mounted

Direct Flexion

You can also ask for flexions when mounted on your horse. Standing at the halt, take an equal feel on both reins with your hands just above the withers. Maintain the pressure until the horse gives—even the smallest give is enough at first—and praise the horse. If you have been able to do flexions successfully while on the ground, the lesson should carry over when you are mounted.

Once the horse gives in the jaw you can prolong the flexion and move forward in the walk, later in the trot, and eventually in the canter, with the horse holding a relaxed contact with your hand and moving forward into the contact. The horse should always feel that the door in front is open for him to move forward.

The horse should be able to stretch in the walk....

...and the trot...   *...and the canter.*

Keeping an elastic contact is essential for the transmission of impulsion through the horse's body. I often will take hold of the reins when teaching a clinic and am astounded at how rigid the rider's arm can be.

If you want the horse to accept the bit and remain light, you must have some give in your arm muscles and in your fingers. Think of the rein as starting at your shoulder. The entire length of your arm must remain pliable and relaxed if you expect the horse to relax his jaw.

Using one rein, ask the horse to flex the jaw to one side and then the other.

Lateral Flexion

Once you get the direct flexion, ask the horse to relax his poll and jaw and move his head to one side or the other. You want to be able to make the horse just move his head and jaw without moving his entire neck. This

will come from a very slight pressure of the reins. The inside rein asks the horse to rotate his jaw to the side and the outside rein should be held upwards to prevent the horse from tilting the head and to prevent the neck from moving. Here again if you have taught this from the ground it will not be too difficult to obtain from the horse's back.

Flexing the Neck

You can also ask the horse to flex his entire neck to one side or the other. The inside rein asks for the flexion and the outside rein controls the amount of bending. The neck is amazingly flexible and the horse can bring his head all the way around to your foot on each side.

Ask the horse to flex deeply to one side and then the other to loosen the neck and poll.

I use this as an exercise when I get on. I have a horror of horses that move off as soon as the rider puts a foot in the stirrup so all my horses learn to wait for a reward when I get on. I carry sugar or a treat in my pocket and the horse quickly learns to anticipate the treat and the head will come around to my foot first on one side then the other. Maybe my horses are spoiled but I achieve a good stretch to each side before we even start work and they stand still to be mounted.

I once watched a clinic given by John Lyons, and what did he do when he got on? He brought the horse's head around to his foot on either side. He didn't give a treat, but the training principle is exactly the same.

Use a treat to get your horse to really stretch to one side.

Stretching the Neck

You can show your horse the way to the ground from the saddle. Begin at the halt. Raise both of your hands and put a steady pressure upward on both sides of the mouth raising the horse's head. It may seem like a contradiction to raise the head when you are trying to get the horse to lower it, but the horse will figure out that the way to escape this pressure is to lower and stretch the neck. It is up to you to be quick to relax the pressure at the slightest offer on the horse's part to stretch down.

A relaxing stretch at the halt.

After a few seconds the horse will lower the neck to relieve the pressure. Your hands must soften but not throw the contact away. You can work on this until the horse will stretch out and down as you relax the contact.

A word of warning, in the beginning stages you may find that your horse tries backing away from the contact, it goes without saying that you need to keep your legs firmly on the horse's sides to prevent him from escaping backwards. That is not what you are asking and the horse must understand this from the start.

Once the horse has realized what you are after, you can do this exercise at the walk, trot, and eventually at the canter. Lo and behold, your horse will give you a perfect stretchy circle in the tests that the judges will reward with high marks.

Working with One Rein

For horses that have a very stiff jaw on one side you can try the following exercise. Take just the rein on the softer side of the mouth; drop the other rein entirely. If you are holding the left rein, lead the horse around to the left in the walk, using just a small pressure and a leading or open rein. Your inside leg is at the girth and the outside leg a little back.

Next, try to change over and ride a right hand circle using the left rein. You will probably need to place the left rein quite high up the neck and push on the neck to turn the horse's head slightly to the right. If you pull

Hold the right rein only and turn to the right.

Raise the rein until it is close to the head and push gently against the neck to turn the head left.

The horse is turning to the left from the pressure of the right rein.

You can help by leaning a bit in the direction you want the horse to move.

too hard the horse will keep turning left. Think of pushing the head over and then letting the horse follow his head. It takes a little practice, but you should be able to ride a loop to the left followed by a loop to the right, using just the one rein. Once you can do this, change and take just the right rein and do the same exercise. Turn to the right then try and turn to the left.

The value here is that you work one side of the mouth independent of the other and the horse can learn to relax his jaw. He cannot set himself against just one rein: he can only lean on you if you take both reins. Don't cheat in this exercise; take the time to make it work for you and your horse. You probably won't want to do this for more then a week but it can be a valuable tool for both you and your horse.

When I learned this exercise, it was quite an eye opener to realize just how important the outside rein can be in turning the horse and I have never had a problem with circles and pirouettes since. I learned to turn my horses with the outside bearing rein against the shoulder and neck instead of relying on the inside rein.

This exercise gives a whole new meaning to change the rein! Now pick up the left rein and repeat the exercise to the other side.

Push the head to the right...

...and the horse turns to the right from the left rein.

2

The Work in Hand

Before you even get on your horse, you can establish your control and work on your horse's submission from the ground. For me, the work in hand and lunging are indispensable to any training program. Your horse must pay attention to you on the ground and respect your space and your authority. You need to establish the "pecking order" right from the start. That is as basic as having your horse move over in the stall or when being groomed and tacked up. The horse should move away from a touch of the hand on his flank. This is a basic requirement. If you expect your horse to move from your leg (or the spur) when you are mounted, you can teach this from the ground. You expect the same response.

This work can be part of your daily routine but should not take more than 10 or 15 minutes at the most. The great advantage is that once you get on your horse he is already in work mode and you do not have to warm up. I try to incorporate some work in hand every day during most of the first year's training, and use it when I am working on the more collected work in subsequent years. Work in hand can be useful at any time during the training process.

To work a horse in hand all you need is a bridle and a whip. If your horse is nervous of the whip, take the time to educate him to accept it. Some horses have been mistreated and develop a real fear of the whip. You have to have a great deal of patience and persistence to overcome this phobia. Carry the whip close to the horse and let him sniff it. Gradually bring the whip closer until you can rub it up and down the neck and shoulder. Do not tap with the whip at this point, just get so you can rub it over the neck and then over the legs and belly and down the hindquarters.

It may take you a week or so before the horse gets used to this. Do as much as you can and try to get a little further each day. For a normal horse one session will usually suffice and you can stop as soon the horse realizes that the whip is non-threatening.

Once the horse accepts the touch of the whip all over you can begin to do the exercises. Do not try to do them all at once; one new thing at a time is the rule when training a horse. They learn by repetition, and they learn by learning, so once they learn the first thing, you can do that each time you work, and add new ideas one at a time.

The exercises are progressive, so do them in the order they are listed. This is so that the horse has a chance to develop his acceptance and learns to become aware of his body and muscles.

I am still not sure why the work in hand is so effective, but it gives you a real domination over the horse, part of the herd ethic we read so much about. You are establishing your authority by showing the horse he has to respect you and to concentrate on moving where and when you want him to. I find it fascinating that most of the so-called natural horsemen, Ray Hunt, Pat Parelli, John Lyons, Monty Roberts use very similar exercises working horses from the ground, bearing out the theory that good horse-manship is universal.

Turning Around the Forehand

The first exercise is to ask the horse to move a hind leg away from the touch of the whip. Stand on the left side of the horse facing the rear. Hold onto the left rein with your left hand and carry the whip in your right

Hold the rein loosely in your left hand and tap the hind leg with the whip to move the horse away from you.

Face the hind leg and step toward it so that the horse moves around you.

hand. Lay the whip across your palm so that you hold it like a fencing foil; it is easier to keep it stabilized. You might have to practice this until you feel comfortable in your control of the whip.

Touch the horse's left hind leg with the whip just below the hock. You want the horse to rotate around you by moving his hind end away from you.

Essentially you are teaching a turn around the forehand. Until the horse understands what you want you may have to tap several times before he moves away from the whip. Just keep insisting. You do not have to use a lot of force just be consistent. Some horses will fly away from the touch of the whip the first time. If this is the case, position yourself near a wall or a fence to prevent the horse from completely escaping you. Some, on the other hand, do not show any reaction at all and you must be more insistent.

As soon as you get even one step, stop and praise the horse so he understands the lesson. The other reaction you might get is that the horse kicks out against the touch of the whip. In this case you have to use the whip again immediately and scold the horse with a loud voice to show this reaction is not to be tolerated. Keep putting the pressure on until the horse stops kicking. Do not give in until the horse realizes you mean business.

The horse should stay relaxed with the neck stretched downward. You can actually watch the muscles of the neck loosen. You can return to this exercise after teaching the horse new movements and use it as a reward and moment of relaxation

Once you can get a few steps moving away from you on the left side, switch sides and work on the right side. Hold the right rein with your right hand and hold the whip in your left hand. Do exactly the same thing. But remember, just because the horse has understood the lesson on one side does not mean he will carry this over to the other side. You must begin again on the other side as if it were a new exercise. Keep at it until you have successfully moved the horse several steps on each side. This is enough for the first day. Go ahead and ride your horse in whatever work you have planned.

The next day, begin again with this exercise and see if you can get the horse to make a complete circle around you on each hand. If it goes well, you can then stop and go ahead with your regular work. If the horse is still apprehensive on the second day, make progress slowly and be patient. Be satisfied with one or two steps on each side.

You can also use the whip on the stomach muscles just behind the girth, this helps the horse to lift his ribcage and free up the forearm. By doing this you also build in a response to pressure from your leg when mounted. Horses have a bunch of reflex muscles in their flank and you are educating those reflexes to respond to a light touch.

Once your horse turns easily around you on each side you can begin the next lesson.

Shoulder-In

For this exercises, use a fence or a wall to help you keep the horse under control. If you do this exercise out in the middle of the field the horse will learn to escape you by taking his hind end too far away and you will wind up back on the circle around you. You need to position your horse along the wall or fence so that the hindquarters are kept on the track by the barrier.

For this exercise position your horse facing left along the wall with the shoulders off the track the hind legs on the track. Stand facing forward beside the horse's left shoulder, holding the left rein in your left hand with your hand close to the bit. The left rein is the inside rein and the right rein is the outside rein. This exercise will help you understand the importance of the outside rein. The horse needs to step towards the outside rein and into that contact.

Face forward and step toward the shoulder. The horse should take contact with the outside rein across the neck.

The left hand will control the position of the head so it needs to be as close as possible to the nose. Bring the right rein across the wither and hold it in your right hand just behind the girth where your heel would be if you were mounted. You hold the whip in this hand also.

This all sounds very complicated and takes some practice to become coordinated with the reins and whip. The most important point is to keep your hands well separated and your shoulders relaxed and open. Many people tend to draw their hands together and this makes the whole exercise quite difficult. Hold the whip horizontally along the horse's flank. Tap the horse on the flank and step towards the shoulder.

The horse will be bent around you, but should step away from you. Try not to pull the left rein back towards you; in fact you can almost push your hand under the horse's chin to move it away from you. You want the horse to move out of your space, not lean towards you. If you run into problems at the beginning, you can always put the horse back onto a circle around you and start over when you get back to the wall.

Once you can successfully get several steps with the horse giving in his neck and maintaining a slight bend around you, stop and make a fuss of him. Remember to *make haste slowly* and give the horse a chance to understand just what it is you are after. Force has no part in this. You cannot force a 1200-pound animal into a preconceived shape. Give the horse time to figure it out. After a few tries you will find the neck and jaw relax and become soft and supple and the horse is beginning to learn to come onto the bit and to carry himself. The key to this exercise is getting the hind legs to cross and step under the body.

Again, do not belabor the point. Once the horse has given you some good steps with little resistance, stop and begin to work on the opposite side. Don't forget the praise. The best reward is to stop the moment you achieve a good result. Equally, if the horse shows resistance you must instantly berate him with your voice and use a firm tap of the whip.

You will probably find that on one side or the other the horse tends to lean on his shoulder and towards you. If this happens, take your whip and using the butt end, jab the shoulder until the horse moves away from you.

This is the result of not keeping your inside hand out from your body far enough. The horse is tipping his head; his ears are no longer level.

The horse has bent his neck too much because the outside rein lacks tension. You lose the effect of the exercise when this happens.

I cannot stress enough that if the horse is to realize his actions are wrong, you must correct him instantly. Horses do not reason; they are instinctive and highly reactive. You must learn to react as quickly. It is as easy to teach a horse the wrong thing as it is to teach him the right thing. Be very sure of what you are trying to accomplish.

As with any work, it is the daily repetition that enables the horse to learn. If you do these exercises just once in a while you will essentially be beginning again each time. It is the daily application of the exercise that enables the horse to understand.

Once the horse has learned an exercise however, it is there for life as they have great memories.

Turn Around the Haunches

Often horses will resist this new idea—you must be patient.

Once you can do the shoulder-in exercise along the wall on both sides with your horse bent around you but moving away from the direction of the bend, you can progress to doing a circle in shoulder-in.

The next step is to teach the horse to bend in the opposite direction and to move into the bend.

Stand on the horse's left side with your left hand close to the bit and your right hand holding the right rein over the wither.

Begin to push the head away to change the bend.

A successful change of bend. Stand more in front of the horse in this exercise.

Gradually pull down on the right rein and push your left hand underneath the horse's jaw to push his head away from you to make him assume a right bend. Keep the whip on the flank to hold the hindquarters in place. Walk towards the horse's head and try to make him walk in a circle bent away from you so he turns around the hindquarters with the outside hind stepping across the inside hind.

It is harder for the horse to bend in this exercise so you may well get some resistance. Work at it by degrees; be content with little bend at the beginning, as the horse develops more suppleness you can increase the bend. Do not try to make the circle too small in the early stages.

Half Pass

The head is too high, but the horse can now begin to develop a half pass.

To begin this exercise, ask for shoulder-in on the short side of the arena and bring the horse onto the centerline. As you reach the centerline, change the bend by pushing the head away with your left hand under the chin, and drawing your right hand down. Your horse should already know how to do this from the previous exercise. Tap the hindquarters away from you. This is difficult until the horse catches on but persevere. It is easier to do this from the centerline towards the wall, as the horse will naturally be drawn back to the track. I find that I position myself a little more forward for this exercise so I can push the forehand away from me. The horse changes from bending around me to bending away from me.

Again this will not happen all at once, you have to work at it in small doses until the horse develops the suppleness to be able to do this. Remember that it takes time to develop muscles.

Engaging Circle

Stand beside the horse facing the hindquarters holding the left rein in the left hand. Take the whip in your right hand and tap the horse on the left hock and step towards him. You want the horse to revolve around you in trot crossing over the inside hind.

Move the horse around at the trot, tapping on the top of the hindquarters.

It amazes me how far under the hind leg can step. This exercise builds the muscles of the hind leg by making the horse really bend and engage. It is a great way to build the strength you will later need for piaffe. You want to keep yourself moving on a small circle, stepping towards the horse's haunches. Keep the arm holding the rein well extended to give the horse room to move around you. There is often a tendency to draw the arm too close to the body.

A word of warning: this exercise will make you quite dizzy! If you want the horse to cross over more, use your whip on the hock or gaskin. If you want the horse to "sit" more and really use his back and bend the joints of the hip, stifle and hock, tap on top of the croup.

This is quite strenuous for the horse so remember to take it easy and not to ask for too much at the beginning. Build muscles, don't strain them.

Rein Back

Position your horse on the track beside the wall and stand slightly in front of him. With your left rein ask the horse to step back. If the horse does not respond, use your whip on the chest. As soon as you get one or two steps, stop and praise the horse. Use your body language by leaning towards the horse's body. As soon as you can get three or four steps,

Ask the horse to step back by walking toward him. This horse has hollowed out, a normal reaction the few times you try.

Keep walking toward the horse until he accepts the idea.

Reverse your direction and go backward, asking the horse to come forward.

A much rounder outline as the horse understands the exercise.

reverse the backwards steps by leaning back and backing up yourself drawing the horse forward toward you. Take the horse forward for three or four steps. Stop and praise the horse.

You want to be able to rock the horse several steps back and immediately go forward again in the same rhythm. Pat Parelli has an exercise called the "yo-yo" that is almost identical except it is done on a long rope. You want to be able to switch from forward to back to forward without pause. As the horse backs up, he engages his hind legs more and more. This is great preparation for piaffe in hand later on.

Spanish Walk

Some horses are restricted in their shoulders; they do not seem able to reach forward well. For these horses I have found that teaching the Spanish walk can loosen the muscles of the shoulder and back. This is an exercise that can be taught once the horse has been worked in the other exercises in hand. I have used this for only about ten horses in my forty years of training, but think that it is a useful exercise for really tough cases

All you need in the way of equipment is a long piaffe type whip, the bridle and a cavesson with a short rein. By using the cavesson you avoid pulling on the horse's mouth to restrain it.

Begin by placing the horse along the side of the ring. It is much easier to do this against the wall or rail so the horse cannot move away from you. Stand in front of the horse holding a long whip in your right hand and holding the left rein close to the bit. Begin by tapping the horse just behind the fetlock. Your aim is to get the horse to pick up his foot.

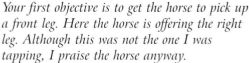

Your first objective is to get the horse to pick up a front leg. Here the horse is offering the right leg. Although this was not the one I was tapping, I praise the horse anyway.

The horse picks up the leg but does not bring it forward as yet.

Once you can get the horse to pick up his foot, your next aim is to get him to stretch that entire leg forward, and then to step onto the outstretched leg.

If tapping behind the fetlock does not get the result, try tapping behind the knee or on the tendon. You have to experiment with each horse to see which spot is best. The aim is to get the horse to pick up the leg and extend it forward.

Once you have reached that point, which may take a week or so, you then must persuade the horse to step forward onto the stretched leg. If you are standing in front of the horse, step backward and pull the horse towards you as he picks up the leg. This takes good coordination on your part! Ideally you want the horse to stretch forward and then place his foot on the ground at the furthest point of the stretch. This will not happen all at once; you must be patient and give the horse time to understand this new request.

The horse must stretch his leg forward and step onto it. It is important that the horse step forward with the hind leg as well; otherwise you just get a horse that is stretching the leg up and forward but not engaging the hind leg. After you can get the horse to make this move with the left leg, turn the process around and start on the right side. At the beginning stage it is enough for the horse just to pick up one leg at a time.

Once the horse is able to stretch either leg, ask him to march forward stretching one leg and then the other. Tap the leg nearest you and then, as the horse lifts that leg, reach under and tap the far leg so you get two or three consecutive steps with lifted legs. The horse will develop a real

swing. You must ensure he keeps stepping forward with the hind legs at the
same time You have to be quick with
your whip and you also have to keep
stepping backwards yourself. I know
that I am not always quick enough and
have been struck on the knee as my
horse makes the required gesture.

The horse stretches the leg and is stepping forward with the hindleg. An exceptional stretch.

The benefits of the Spanish Walk
for the horse are many: his shoulder
muscles are stretched and his back is
developed from the stretch through his
midsection. Look at the photos to see
which muscles are being worked.

Once the horse has mastered this exercise from the ground, you can
ask the horse do this while you are mounted. It is just a matter of tapping the horse with the whip on his forearm when you are in the saddle.
Use the whip where the leg and the shoulder meet. I also raise the rein
on one side and then the other. I find that putting my leg far forward on
the side of the stretch enables the horse to move without any restriction.
Just be careful not to do this too much as it may well come back to haunt
you in the ring. If you have watched the videos of the Olympic dressage
competition in Greece, you can see the Spanish horse Invasor offer a step
of Spanish Walk in the middle of his walk work. So be careful.

By working on these exercises before you climb on your horse, you give
the horse a chance of understanding how to move his body and legs without the added difficulty of the rider's weight on his back. You are building
communication.

These seven exercises can be taught early in the training of any horse
and revisited whenever necessary. I find the work in hand helps me understand each horse and to study his reactions to new demands. Later, there
is additional work you can include when teaching the piaffe and passage.

3
Putting Your Horse on the Aids

Once your horse has been prepared by five to ten minutes of the work in the preceding chapters, you are ready to get down to the daily training under saddle.

Some horses need to be ridden firmly forward at the beginning of a training session while others benefit from suppling at the walk. Personally, I like to be sure my horse is responsive and on the aids before asking for very forward work. It is also important that you give the horse's muscles a chance to stretch before asking anything energetic. This is even more important for an older horse

Once you are in the saddle, expect the horse to accept an elastic contact and be ready to move forward into it. You do this by asking for the direct flexion discussed in Chapter 1. As soon as the horse yields his jaw, move him forward from the pressure of your leg, maintaining an elastic feel on the mouth. You should be able to go from halt to walk without any change in the horse's head and neck position. If your horse ignores the leg aid, remind him with the whip that you mean business.

Do not be content with a bad transition; this is the basis for all your transitions and the horse must concentrate and be willing to respond. If his head goes up, or he jumps forward with a tense back, take the time to repeat the transition until you get the correct answer to your aids.

The horse should step freely forward from the halt.

This is very important: you must insist from the very beginning that the horse give you a prompt and willing transition.

Nor should you be content with resistance or laziness. Repeat as often as it takes to get the correct response. Horses are creatures of habit and they need to be told what is appropriate and what is not tolerated. Your transitions need to be "seamless" in that they should just happen.

To move your horse from your leg, a light pressure is all that should be needed. You should not sit on the horse's back with a death grip with both legs. All you achieve is a tightening of the horse's sides and reflexes, making communication much more difficult. The horse needs to learn to move forward from a slight pressure of the calf muscles. Horses that have to be ridden with strong leg aids have been taught to rely on strength and force, rather than on subtle aids.

When I learned to ride, I was taught to grip with the thigh and calf and, consequently, my horses tended to be heavy and required a lot of strength to get moving. I was fortunate enough to go to Portugal and ride at the school of Nuno Oliveira in Avessada, a small village just north of Lisbon. I fancied myself a pretty strong rider at that point; after all, I was eventing at the intermediate level on a huge, strong Canadian half-bred and had developed legs and arms of iron.

I was chagrined to find I could not get the horses in the school to go forward. The harder I tried, the less they went. After a week or so, I found that if I relaxed my legs and gave quick soft aids, the horses became delightfully responsive and I was no longer exhausted when I finished my ride. You can teach a horse to be light and you can teach a horse to be heavy. Light is better.

I find that five to ten minutes spent at the walk at the beginning of a session ensures that the horse is attentive and over his feet before you begin the real work of the day.

Riding a Square: Square Serpentines

I usually start out by riding a square in the walk. I have my horse walking on contact and make a quarter turn to the left by using the outside rein on the neck and shoulder. I use my inside leg at the girth with the outside leg back to prevent the hindquarters from stepping out. A horse prefers to turn like a boat. If you

Beginning the turn, the horse bent around the inside leg and the shoulders coming to the left.

turn the head in one direction often the hindquarters will go in the opposite direction and the horse avoids bending and stepping up under himself.

Try to turn the horse from the outside aids. The inside rein indicates the direction by going a little toward your inside knee, but your outside rein has the job of bringing the horse's body in the new direction. Walk on for about 10 meters and ride another a quarter turn. If you do this correctly you are making the horse step under himself and engage his hindquarters.

The rhythm must stay the same both on the straightaway and during the turns; do not allow any variation. The horse must not slow down to make things easier for himself. He must keep the same march during the entire time. You can throw in a couple of halts along the way. This is the perfect way to check if your horse is straight. The horse should neither fall in on his shoulder or

Riding a Square

Turning to the right, the outside hind leg crosses over the inside hind leg.

The horse has shortened his neck and the turn is not balanced.

This is an exercise that can be done in the warm up arena before a test.

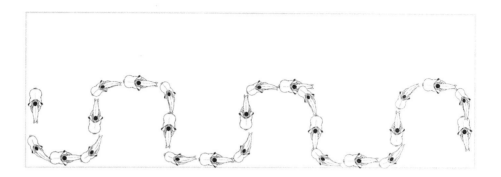

The Square Serpentine

allow his quarters to fall out. Once you are content with the left handed square, change over and do a square to the right.

While doing this exercise it goes without saying the horse needs to be thinking and marching forward, not dragging his feet. The whole object is to get him to move over his feet with rhythm and energy. Each step must be like the one before. Even in the turns the rhythm must stay the same; that is the difficult bit.

If your horse is balanced and soft you can enlarge on this exercise by riding a square serpentine down the entire school. Do two turns to the left followed by two turns to the right. Make sure the turns are real quarter turns on the spot without slowing the rhythm.

How long you stay in this exercise depends upon your horse on any given day. If he does a nice balanced square in each direction, remains straight and rhythmical, and is light on the rein, you can go on to other things. If, on the other hand, you are missing some of these components, stay at the square serpentine until you get a good response.

Leg Yielding

The object of the leg yield is to get the horse to move away from the leg pressure and to cross his legs. By getting this crossing you are asking the horse to bend and flex his joints more than he would if he just went straight. Any time a horse brings a hind leg under and across the other hind leg, you are working on the bending of the joints and increasing the amount of engagement of the hindquarter.

Leg yielding is the first of the lateral movements and is used to prepare the horse for more advanced lateral work. If you have been doing the work in hand the horse already has the idea of moving sideways from the pressure of the whip. You can now transfer that idea over into his moving from the pressure of your leg.

Begin by going to the left on a 20-meter circle in the walk. In the vicinity of the centerline of your arena, bring the horse's head, neck and shoulder towards the left but ask him to move to the right, away from your left leg. Sit slightly heavier on your left seat bone to drive the horse to the right. However, if you sit too much on the inside, you will be blocking the movement.

Push from the left seat bone toward the right seat bone with a small rocking motion to draw the horse to the right. In the walk, the horse moves his legs in broken diagonals, left front, right hind, right front, left hind. To move the left hind, time your left leg aid as the horse steps onto the right front. This gives the horse time to accept and respond to the aid just as the left hind leg leaves the ground; he can then cross it over the right hind.

Take a moment to think about how a horse reacts. When you give an aid, your brain thinks about the aid and tells your body what to do. Your body then gives the aid, the horse's body receives the aid and tells the horse's brain. The horse's brain then translates the aid and tells his body how to move.

The horse remains straight in his body and neck and moves over from the right leg, away from the rail.

The horse moves back to the rail from the left leg.

You must go through that whole sequence before the horse is able to respond. It takes much longer to describe this process than to actually do it. The horse's reflexes are lightening quick and the transmission of the signals is quick, but there is always a slight delay in between the time you give an aid and get the response. It stands to reason you should time your aid precisely so that the leg or body part you want to move can respond.

A horse can only move a leg as it comes off the ground; you must recognize that moment and give your aid just before the leg is in the air. If the horse has all his weight on a particular leg, he cannot move it until the entire sequence of the gait is repeated.

When I first learned to ride no one ever talked about the timing of the aids; you were on your own. Sometimes you hit the appropriate moment and sometimes not. When you train yourself to know where your horse's feet are at each step, you can influence them with ease. The more advanced the horse is in the training the more important it is to time your aids precisely.

If you ask your horse to move a leg when he has all his weight on it, he cannot respond and easily can be confused and resist. To move the left hind leg in walk, your left leg should push at the moment the horse's right front goes forward, and then relax to allow the horse to respond. It is vice versa for the right hind, use the aid as the left front goes forward.

It is a mistake to put a pushing leg on the horse and clamp it there. The horse has no chance to respond and will often just lean against the leg instead of moving away from it. Or the horse will get upset as he does not have a chance to understand what you want. The big secret to giving a good aid is to give it and relax it immediately. Horses are much stronger than we are. The moment you get into a strength battle you are bound to lose out. Try to use more of a nudge with your leg than a long drawn out push.

Leg Yield Down the Wall, Head to the Wall with a Turn on the Forehand

Once your horse has learned to move away from either leg on the circle, you can use this valuable exercise down the wall or long side of your arena. If you do not have an indoor, find a fence line to work against. Once the horse has learned this lesson, you can do it along the arena but the exercise works better if you can find at least a chest-high fence.

Position your horse facing the wall at about a 35-degree angle at the beginning of the long side going to the right. Keeping an elastic contact and ask the horse to move off your left leg and leg yield to the right.

Ask for one step at a time, and it is important to keep the horse's neck straight. For the correct response, you must not let the horse bend his neck to avoid having to step into the contact. You are asking the horse to move from the leg into the opposite hand. The wall will effectively hold the horse for you so you do not need a strong contact. If the horse bumps his head on the wall the first few times you try this, don't worry about it; that is a problem the horse can solve for himself.

Many horses will try to back off from the wall to reduce the pressure. This must not be allowed; use the wall to contain the horse. You will find that after a few steps you begin to get a round outline as the horse drops his nose and rounds up through the neck, and becomes elastic and light on the rein.

At the end of the long side, stop and push the horse's hindquarters around in a turn on the forehand just until he reaches a position that is 35 degrees from the track. Do not make the mistake of letting the horse move his hindquarters all the way to the track: you should be in control of the entire horse at each step. Once you have turned the horse around, repeat the leg yielding down the wall in the opposite direction. One way will be definitely more difficult for the horse than the other, so take your time and let the horse learn to become more supple.

This exercise done well is excellent suppling work and puts the horse into a round and soft shape. Once the horse has learned to do this both ways with ease, add a small circle away from the track while still in leg yield. The horse will now be making a circle with the reverse bend. Continue down the track. When your horse really gives in his neck, you will feel a softness in the contact. Once you have established this, you can bend him towards the arena and trot a 10 to15

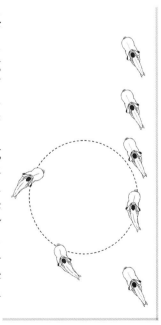

meter circle, maintaining the softness. As you approach the track again, come down to the walk and continue with the leg yield, head to the wall.

The leg yield and the turn serve to soften and prepare the horse to go in the proper balance with the hind leg engaged beneath the body. If you start your work with this preparation you save a lot of time and avoid a lot of resistance in getting your horse on the aids correctly.

4

Making Your Horse More Responsive and Supple

The first chapters deal with getting the horse attentive and responsive—now you need to get moving forward.

After the initial 10 to 15 minutes spent on the earlier exercises in your training session, now begin to work your horse in the trot. By this point in the lesson he should be accepting a good contact and ready to move on.

Alternating Trots

A useful beginning exercise uses a forward rising trot down the long side, with the horse allowed to stretch forward and down. Then, shorten the horse by putting on more leg, taking a fairly strong half halt and ride sitting trot on the short end.

You do not want the horse to slow his rhythm or lose the forward feeling on the short end when you sit. You want instead to compress the horse and create even more energy; use more leg and push the horse into a more compact shape. When you take more feel on the reins,

Ride in rising trot with a downward stretch and active forward motion.

Lengthen down the long side of the arena.   *Shorten the trot to collect the horse.*

you must correspondingly use more leg. When you reach the beginning of the next long side, release the energy you have created by softening your leg aid, and allowing your arms to relax about two inches forward. Soften your leg and your hands and allow the horse to trot on.

In other words, you want to **make** the horse trot on the short end and create lots of energy, and then **allow** the horse to move out with longer, softer strides. You want to have a difference in the shape of the horse and the length of the strides. It does not have to be dramatic but the horse should become adjustable.

Don't keep going the same way all the time. Change the rein across the diagonal in the rising trot, and repeat the exercise going the other way.

Transitions between Gaits

I like to work on transitions at the beginning of a work session to see if the horse is able to transfer more weight onto the hindquarters. I believe that working transitions from trot to walk and back to trot, if done correctly, can help the horse to engage and step through with the hindquarters. I once audited a clinic given by Reiner Klimke, where most of the riders were at the FEI levels. Almost without exception he had them ride on a circle around him at the beginning of the lesson and do transitions from trot to walk to trot until their horses relaxed and began to be round and engaged. It goes without saying that your transitions should be ridden from your seat and leg with only the slightest pressure on the reins so that the horse is ready at any time to move promptly forward again.

Transitions within the Gaits

You should also ride frequent transitions within any given gait, asking the horse to step freely forward and then compressing him by using a fairly strong half halt with your legs, seat and hands, shortening his entire body but producing more energy. This is a step forward from the loosening and softening that you use at the beginning of the warm up under saddle.

Circles within the Circle

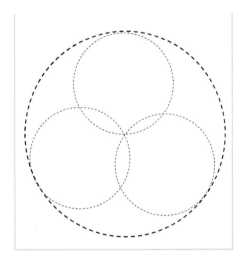

I find it very effective to ride transitions on a 20-meter circle. I ask the horse to go forward on the circle with a longer frame and a stretching of the neck. Then I ask for a 10-meter circle in a shorter frame within the larger circle. You can easily ride three circles within your large circle and the horse begins to anticipate and becomes responsive to the aids. This exercise can be done at trot and canter. Eventually, as the horse progresses, you can dispense with the small circles and merely ask for collection. The advantage of using the small circle is that the circle will actually work for you as the horse begins to anticipate it without your having to use strong aids.

Small Circles to Teach Downward Transitions within a Gait

You can use this training technique when you begin to teach your horse to lengthen his stride on the side of the arena or even across the diagonal. Ask for the lengthening down the long side of the arena with a small circle at the end.

Most dressage tests are written so that the transitions into and back from extended or lengthened movements are awarded a separate mark. If you take the time to teach the horse to adjust his stride and collect easily

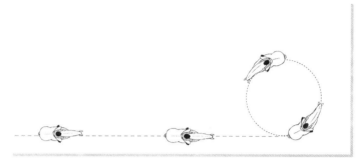

you can gain extra points. As a judge I often find that riders don't seem to have figured this out and show a minimal transition, or none at all, at the end of a lengthening. Don't throw marks away.

More Leg Yielding

Leg yielding is the exercise we do with young horses to begin teaching them the lateral movements. It is equally useful for more advanced horses as a suppling and loosening exercise and can be used in combination with more advanced lateral work as the horse's training progresses.

In the previous chapter the leg yield was discussed as a beginning exercise in the walk both on the circle and down the wall. It can also be used in the trot and eventually in the canter with great benefits for any horse.

Leg Yield on the Spiral

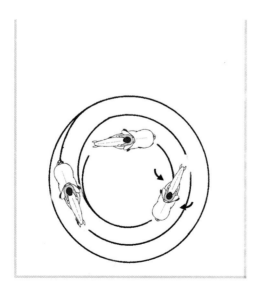

The first exercise I use to teach the horse to leg yield from either leg is the spiral on the circle.

Begin on a 20-meter circle with your horse trotting forward with a good contact. Gradually decrease the size of your circle by using your outside leg slightly back behind the girth and using your outside rein against the wither. Your inside hand can lead the horse into the spiral, but should not pull his head and neck in. Your inside leg should be on the girth as you move into the circle to prevent the horse from falling in. As you decrease your circle, the horse's outside legs will have to take slightly longer steps and the inside pair of legs will have to increase their bending. The smaller the circle the more gymnastic effect it has on your horse.

Usually, in the early stages of training you will not be able to bring the horse onto too small a circle. All too often the horse will leave his hind legs outside the circle. Do not allow this to happen. This is why it is so important for you to use your outside leg to hold the hind legs on the same track as the forelegs, and your outside rein must line the hindquarters up behind the forehand. The smaller the circle gets, the more your outside leg must go back to hold the hindquarters.

Once you have reached a 10-meter circle, reverse the process and ask the horse to move out from your inside leg, which must now move slightly back from the girth. Your outside leg will stay in contact but will allow the inside leg to be the dominant aid. Your hands stay the same. Your outside rein contains the neck and the amount of bending, and the inside rein stays slightly towards the inside. Do not use the inside rein to try and push the neck out; this will only block the flow of energy from the hind leg. Your inside rein must allow the horse to move to the outside but still keep the bend of the circle.

This is an exercise you can go back to at any time to rebalance your horse and make him come through correctly from behind. Later on in your training when you are working in collection, you can ask the horse to decrease the circle in the haunches-in position and increase it in shoulder-in.

Leg Yield from the Quarter Line

The first few times you ask for a straight leg yield in trot, bring the horse onto the quarter line and ask him to move back towards the track. It is probably easier to try this first on the left rein as most horses will go more easily this way. Horses will naturally gravitate towards the wall. Your job is to keep the horse straight in his body and neck and to maintain the rhythm you have. The horse must neither slow down nor speed up in response to the demand. If you use too strong an aid the horse will tend to hurry. You need to use the right or outside rein to keep the horse's shoulder straight and the left or inside leg pulses with the horse's strides. Your outside leg must also remain in contact with the right side of the horse.

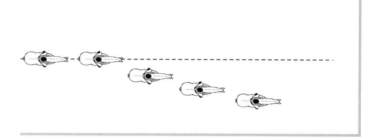

All too often I see riders just using the inside leg and letting the outside leg leave the horse's side. It is important to ride both sides of the horse. One leg aid is the dominant one but the other leg must support it. In the same way the reins must both direct and balance the horse. You cannot hang onto the left rein if you are asking the horse to move to the right. The right rein will remain in a steady contact to keep the horse straight and to prevent any speeding up, and the left rein must soften to allow the horse to move over.

Your seat must remain in the middle of the horse; you must not collapse over your left leg when you ask the horse to move over. You cannot sit with all your weight to the left if you are asking the horse to move under you to the right. I find that if you think about moving from your left seat bone to the right at each step you will be able to help your horse move under you.

You should also turn your head in the direction of the movement. Your head is the heaviest bone in your body and can be used to good effect in directing your horse.

In all leg yielding exercises the aim is to get the horse to move away from your leg and to cross his own legs over underneath the body.

Leg Yield from the Centerline and Straightening

Once the horse has the concept of moving from your leg, you can vary the place where you ask for this exercise.

Turn down the centerline and ask the horse to move back towards the track. Be careful to keep the horse straight, not falling onto either shoulder or overbending the neck. A slight flexion at the poll away from the movement is acceptable.

The rhythm of the gait must remain exactly the same. You can test this by asking the horse to move over a few steps, ride straight forward for a few steps, and then move over again. This ensures that you use both your

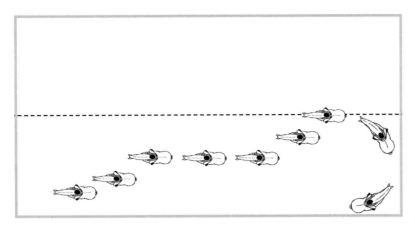

legs and makes the horse responsive and attentive. Try this exercise going both ways in the school. When you ask for a lateral movement you should always be able to ride straight forward at any time with no change of balance or rhythm and without resistance.

Half Diagonal and Leg Yield, Head to Wall

Ride across half the diagonal and ask for a leg yield with the horse's head towards the wall. Here you want to ask for an angle of about 35 degrees, not more, as that would place too much strain on your horse at this stage.

This is an exercise that leads to the haunches-in later on. Up to this point you have asked the horse to move straight down the track, but now you are asking him to bring the haunches inside. The wall will hold the horse effectively so you do not need a strong contact. Your hands should contain the base of the neck between them and the horse must keep the rhythm of his trot as he moves down the school. Your job is to keep the

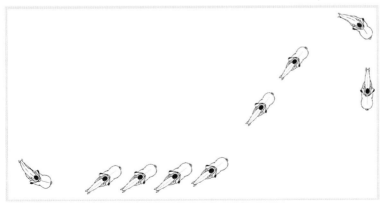

horse straight. At the end of the long side, just before the corner, straighten the horse to pass through the corner onto the short side.

Leg Yield On and Off the Wall

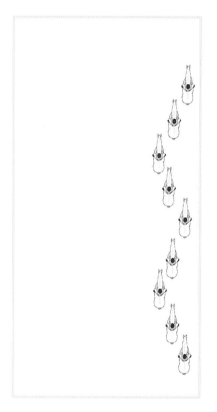

I find this to be a very effective exercise once I can move the horse off either leg.

At the beginning of the long side, ask the horse to move away from the wall two or three steps, reverse your aids and move him back onto the track again. By asking for just a couple of steps and immediately reversing the direction, you effectively move the horse over all four feet. The exercise has tremendous value in balancing the horse.

It is important to keep the horse straight in his body and neck and not allow him to change his rhythm as he moves first one way and then the other. The first few times you try this, you may find that the horse is slow to react. But if you persevere, you will find that his balance gets better and better. This exercise also makes you more quick and accurate with your aids and the horse becomes more and more responsive.

This exercise can be ridden in all three gaits but, of course, you want to start with the walk until the horse understands. Progress to riding it in trot and, when the canter is balanced, try riding it in canter also. It is good preparation for the more advanced exercises we will consider in a future chapter.

The Tight Serpentine

To teach the horse to move off your leg easily and to supple his back, the following exercise is invaluable in any working session. I also use it in the warm up area at shows.

Beginning at the short end of the arena, ask the horse to make many turns off your leg. Ride between the track and the centerline in eight to ten meter loops; the smaller you make the loops the more benefit you get from the exercise. You'll need to push the horse through the change of bend from your leg.

Begin with a left hand loop and your horse bending left. As you begin to move towards the rail, push the horse off your right leg so that you move the horse's body to the left to change the bend. As you go around the loop and start across the school, push the horse with your left leg, pushing his body to the right.

The benefit of using this exercise is that the horse learns to move from each leg in quick succession and, by using your legs to change the bend, the horse goes more forward. If you try and change the bend by just using the reins, you will lose the impulsion instead of creating it as you change the bend.

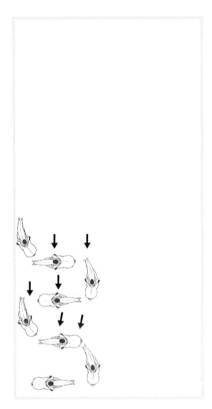

The Tight Serpentine. The arrows show where to begin using your new leg to push the horse's body in the new direction..

5

The Road to Collection:
Better Bending and Balance

Once the leg yield comes easily for your horse, you are ready to begin to work on the lateral movements that bring your horse towards true collection and engagement. Without engagement there can be no collection; the activation and development of the muscles of the hindquarters are the goals. The more weight the horse can transfer to his hind legs the lighter and more maneuverable he becomes. All the lateral work is designed to flex, develop and strengthen the joints of the hindquarters.

Shoulder-In

Shoulder-in is perhaps the most important exercise you teach your horse. Nuno Oliveira said time and time again "Shoulder-in is the aspirin of equitation": you can use it to fix almost all of your problems." Baucher, the inventor of the movement, or the first person to identify it in writing, said in 1842, "Shoulder-in is the first and last lesson you must teach your horse."

The value of the shoulder-in is that it brings the inside hind leg under the horse and increases the suppleness of the entire body. The horse is bent around the inside leg and moves towards the opposite direction. It is easier for the horse to do this than to move in the direction of the bend as he has to later on in the travers, renvers and half pass.

In shoulder-in, the hindquarters are on the track, the shoulders inside and the horse is bent around the inside leg.

You can use a few steps of shoulder-in at any time during your dressage tests to rebalance and prepare your horse for the next movement. You should ride each corner of the arena with a slight shoulder-in feeling so that your horse remains straight and does not fall on his shoulders in the corners or in the turns to the centerline.

Shoulder-In from Leg Yield

One way to teach the shoulder-in is to use your leg yield from the centerline and when you reach the track continue down the track in a shoulder-in. If you leg yield from the left leg toward the center of the long side when you reach the track you can ask the horse to move along the track with a slight bend to the

Top left: Ride the horse in leg yield back to the track.
Bottom left: As you come close to the track begin to develop a bend to the left.
Bottom right: Upon reaching the track, ask for a bend to the left and begin to ride a shoulder-in with the hind legs on the track and the forehand to the inside.

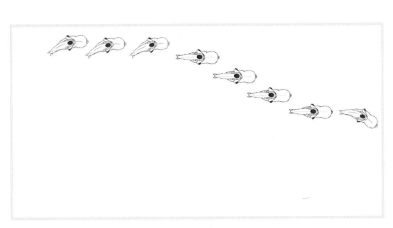

left around your left leg. Your left leg will need to be on the girth while your right leg stays a little behind to prevent the hind legs from stepping out.

Essentially you want the forehand to stay just inside the track while the hind legs move straight down the track. If you do not guard against the hind legs stepping out, you are merely leg yielding down the wall without any bend.

10-Meter Circle to Shoulder-In

Another way to begin is to ride a 10-meter circle just after the corner and, with your horse in position for another circle, ask him to move off your inside leg down the track.

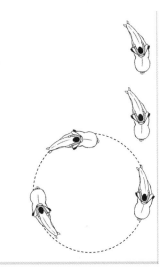

Again, it is easier to teach the concept in the walk before you trying it in trot. At any time during your shoulder-in you should be able to move forward again onto the 10-meter circle. As soon as your horse loses his rhythm or impulsion, allow him to do a circle and ask for the shoulder-in again as you get back to the track. Do not ask for a long period of shoulder-in in the beginning stages; be content with getting a few good steps and reward the horse by allowing him to circle. As the horse understands the demands, you can increase the number of steps until you can ride half of the long side in the exercise.

Shoulder-In and Shoulder-Out on the Circle

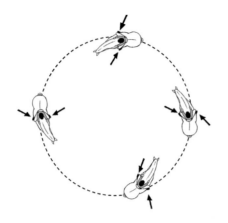

Shoulder-in can be used to good effect on the circle once the horse has developed the ability to maintain his rhythm and impulsion. You can ride a large circle in shoulder-in, change the bend and the driving leg, and ride a shoulder-out on the circle.

If you are going to the left in shoulder-in, your horse will be positioned looking into the circle. His shoulders will be slightly into the circle and he will move off your left leg. Your right leg holds the hind legs on the track of the circle and your outside rein, the right rein, will hold the neck and shoulders into the circle. If you try to do this movement by bringing the head and neck in with the inside rein, you will only succeed in blocking the movement. A true test of the correctness of your shoulder-in will be the ability to release the contact on the inside rein every now and again and have the horse maintain his bend and balance. The energy must travel from the inside hind leg toward the outside rein.

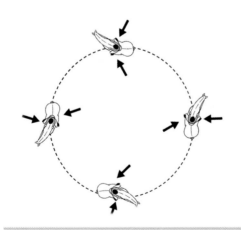

Once you can ride a good circle in the shoulder-in, with a lot of swing and no resistance, you can change the position of your horse and ask for a reverse shoulder-in, a "shoulder-out," on the same circle. Still riding on the left hand circle, gradually bring the horse's head and shoulders to the outside of the circle and bend him around your right leg to ask for the shoulder-out. The horse will now be moving from your right leg into your left rein and looking to the outside of the circle; he is still moving away from the bend.

Haunches-In and Haunches-Out

Haunches-in and haunches-out are actually the same movements; the difference depends on the position of the horse in relation to the track. Once the horse has learned the shoulder-in and can maintain his rhythm and impulsion easily, you can begin to ask for the haunches-in. Instead of the horse being bent away from the direction of the movement, you are now going to ask him to bend and to move in the direction of that bend.

As with shoulder-in and shoulder-out, I find it easiest to teach this movement in the walk so the horse has time to understand the new demand. Ride a 10-meter circle from the track and just before the horse returns to the track, ask him to keep his haunches to the inside.

In other words, do not let the hind leg complete the circle. With your outside leg back, holding the hind legs in, and your inside leg at the girth, maintaining the bend, ride the horse several steps down the track and return to another circle.

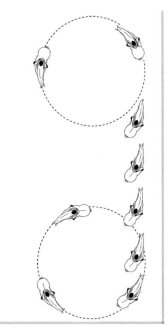

Ideally the forelegs travel down the track and the hind legs will be inside. The important part of the exercise is that the horse maintains the bend in the direction of the movement and brings his hind legs more under his body. You will have to use the outside rein to guard against the shoulder drifting towards the wall.

If that happens, the horse avoids the suppling effect of the movement and will be doing a leg yield instead. Be content with just a few steps in the beginning stages. It is better to do a few good steps and relax and reward the horse, than to try and do too many steps and have the horse resist, lose balance and rhythm, and tighten up. It takes time to develop strength and suppleness. Give your horse a chance to develop his muscles correctly.

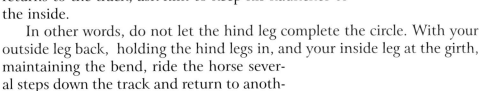

When the horse can easily keep the bend for several steps without resistance, you can progress to asking the exercise in the trot, and then in the canter. Haunches-in is the preparation for the half pass.

Haunches-Out

Once you have developed the haunches-in, reverse your horse's bend and ask him to move with his haunches to the outside of the track and the forehand on the inside. Coming out of the corner on the left rein, ask your horse to bring his forehand off the track and bend around your right leg with his haunches to the outside. Ask for a few steps and straighten again.

This exercise requires concentration from you and your horse, but it is the same exercise as the haunches-in, just with the opposite positioning. The exercise itself is the same in terms of bend and aids and development of suppleness. The horse is around your inside leg (the inside leg of the bend not of the arena) and the outside rein holds the shoulders and envelops the horse.

In haunches-out, the horse is bent around the right leg with the haunches toward the rail, maintaining a right bend.

Haunches-In on the Centerline

Once the horse understands these movements you can use them to good effect by riding haunches-in on the centerline or the quarter lines. In the exercise you are forced to carry the horse on your inside leg to keep

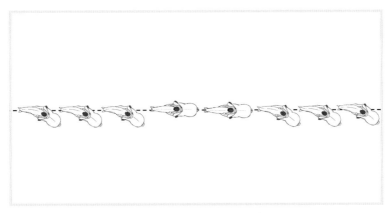

Haunches-In on the Centerline

the line; this is valuable in teaching you to do the more advanced work with perfect straightness.

Ride your horse onto the centerline, and ask him for haunches-in. In this movement the front legs will remain on the centerline and the haunches will be off the line. Ride about a third of the line in haunches-in, straighten the horse onto the centerline for another third of the way and ask for haunches-in again. By riding the haunches-in, straightening and haunches-in again you will find both you and your horse must concentrate on where you are in the arena. This is a tremendous exercise for improving suppleness and responsiveness.

Haunches-In to Medium Trot to Haunches-In, on the Centerline

The next exercise in this progression is to ride down the centerline in haunches-in, straighten the horse and ask for some steps of medium trot, recollect and ask for haunches-in again. This exercise is more advanced and will help you achieve those transitions within the gait that are so important they receive a separate mark in the FEI tests.

Alternating Shoulder-In and Haunches-In

To make your horse responsive and agile, alternate shoulder-in and haunches-in, on a straight line or on a circle. Ride shoulder-in on a quarter of a circle, swing the horse around your inside leg and ride haunches-in for the next quarter circle. Swing the horse back into the shoulder-in for the next quarter and so on. Ridden with attention to maintenance of the

rhythm and impulsion, this exercise is excellent for developing collection.

The exercise can be ridden in trot and in canter, where it improves the horse's balance and engagement if ridden correctly.

As with all the lateral exercises, take things slowly and do not ask for too much at the beginning. Give your horse time to understand and to develop the necessary muscle tone.

The time you spend doing lateral work should be interspersed with vigorous forward riding down the long sides and across the diagonal, so you do not lose that all-important forward feeling.

Alternating shoulder-in and haunches-in on the circle.

Combining Lateral Exercises

I sometimes ride a circle in shoulder-in, change and ride the same circle in haunches-in, change the bend and ride the same circle in shoulder-out, put the haunches outside and ride haunches-out. This can be especially useful in a warm up area where you have limited space and time to prepare before going into the ring. By riding each side of your horse in this way, you can check to be sure you have your horse in front of your aids.

Rein Back

The rein back is an exercise to be used with great care. It certainly helps to develop the bending of the quarters, but you must take the time to develop it carefully. If the horse has been worked in hand in the rein back, he should be able to understand the exercise from the saddle.

From the halt, keep the contact and ask the horse to move from your leg; create the energy, but do not allow the horse to move forward. If you lean slightly forward (about the only time in riding you want to lean forward), your seat bones will be lighter, allowing the horse to move back.

Use alternate aids with the reins and your legs as soon as the horse moves backward, stepping with the horse rather than just pulling him backward. As soon as you get even one step back, stop the demand and praise the horse before asking for more steps. The rein back is an exercise that is seldom done well at the lower levels because riders tend to use too much hand trying to force the horse backward. The horse must move back with a rounded back, not drop out from under you and become hollow. It is imperative to keep the horse straight. Most horses will try to evade the bending of the hind leg by moving the haunches in or out so the rein back becomes crooked.

If you have a great deal of trouble with this exercise, enlist the help of a friend to stand at the horse's head. The person on the ground can tap the horse's chest gently with the whip to indicate what is necessary. As I said, if the horse could do this in hand, he will be able to do it with you on board.

Turn on the Haunches and Half Pirouette

Once your horse can do these early lateral movements at the walk, you can teach the horse to do the half pirouette in walk. The difference between a half turn on the haunches and the half pirouette is that the half pirouette is done out of collected walk.

In the beginning, ask the horse to do a turn on the haunches from the medium walk. This is a movement that many riders seem to have great difficulty in performing correctly. The horse gets stuck on the spot, loses the rhythm, turns around the middle, or even worse, steps back because of too much tension on the rein.

There are some useful exercises to avoid these pitfalls. The turn on the haunches and pirouette should always be ridden out of the walk and not from a halt. Without impulsion it is just about impossible for the horse to step around the turn correctly.

Turn on the Haunches From a Volte

For this exercise, put your horse on a small circle, a volte, in the walk. Begin to ride the volte and then bring the shoulders into the middle of the circle using both hands to bring the shoulders around. If you have been riding your squares successfully, the aids are the same; you just ask for four or five steps instead of two. You lead the horse around; do not try to pull him around.

Your outside leg prevents the haunches from stepping out of the turn.

Turn on the Haunches from a Half Pass

While we'll discuss half pass exercises in more detail later on, I want to mention its usefulness in the turn on the haunches. I find that if you ride a half pass in walk coming off the track towards the centerline, you can easily ask for a half turn as you near the centerline. After the half turn, continue the half pass back along the same line. By concentrating on the half pass, it is easier to keep a better rhythm to the steps of the hind legs.

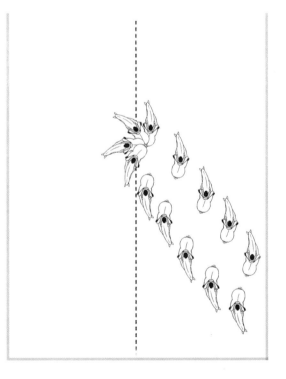

Turn from the Trot

It is not possible to ride a turn on the haunches or pirouette from the trot, but you can still ride the turn in conjunction with the trot. Ride around the short end of the arena in trot, make a transition to the walk and after two or three steps ask for a turn and proceed immediately in the trot again. This is another excellent schooling exercise used by the German school and called the "short turn." The exercise increases engagement and is useful in preparing the half passes.

Entwickeln On and Off the Wall, Advanced

In Chapter Three I included the leg yield on and off the wall as an exercise to improve the horse's attention and balance. Now that the horse can perform lateral work with some degree of collection, you can use the following exercise not found in any tests but having tremendous value in your training routine. The German word for this exercise is *entwickeln* and, as with many of the foreign dressage terms, is difficult to translate exactly.

It can mean beginning, developing, evolving, generating and producing, but no matter what you call it, the exercise is of immense benefit to your horse.

Shoulder-In On and off the Wall

Begin in the walk. Ride shoulder-in on the long side on the left rein; the majority of horses are easier on this side. Come out of the corner with the horse bent around your left leg and ask for a couple of steps of shoulder-in down the track. Now straighten your horse and ride two or three steps forward as if you were going to change rein across the arena.

Bend your horse around your inside leg again and ride in shoulder-in position back to the track. Continue down the track for a couple of steps, straighten, go forward two or three steps, and again ride back to the track in shoulder-in.

The most important part of this exercise is to do the entire movement in the same rhythm and balance. When you first try it, you will probably only be able to do three or four repetitions down the length of the arena. Once you and the horse get the hang of it, you should be able to do about ten repetitions on the long side.

Shoulder-In On and Off the Wall

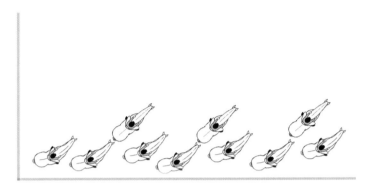

When you straighten the horse, you must straighten by using the outside rein and leg so that the horse's shoulders remain in the same position relative to the wall.

With practice you will figure out just what it takes for each individual horse to understand and be quick to answer the aids as you change from one mode to the other. You do not want to belabor the point by using this exercise for an extended period; use some relaxing moments in between the demands made by this exercise.

Once you can manage this in walk, you can progress to the trot and then eventually to the canter.

Travers (Haunches-In) On and Off the Wall

This is a progression from the exercise in shoulder-in; now ride the same exercise in *travers* position. Beginning on the left rein, ride *travers* out of the corner and on a slight diagonal line into the arena, ride two or three steps, straighten and ride back toward the wall.

When the horse reaches the track, change back to the travers and ride into the arena again for two or three steps. The diagrams will help to clarify this movement. This exercise is excellent for improving your horse's response and agility.

Travers On and Off the Wall

Renvers (Haunches-out) On and Off the Wall

Contrary to what you have been doing with most exercises, this one should start by going on the right rein. Most horses bend more easily to the left and in *renvers* to the right you will be using the left bend.

This exercise begins with asking your horse to move onto the diagonal line. After two or three steps, ask for a left bend around your left leg and bring the horse in renvers back towards the track. Straighten and ride into the arena again for a couple of steps and come back to the track. In this exercise the danger is that the horse will drift back to the track with the shoulders first. Your inside leg has to hold the bend and prevent this from happening

In these last exercises the value is in being able to change from one demand to the other in rapid succession without any loss of impulsion or collection.

It is not going to happen all at once; it will take some time to work these exercises out so that the horse can reap the full benefit.

A word of caution: remember to take your horse out for a hack once in a while as a break from the demands of the ring. Nothing sours a horse as much as continual drilling. Horses were not created to go round and round a 20 by 60 meter arena. They need to get out into the open and go up and down hills as well.

Renvers On and Off the Wall

Half Pass

The half pass can be developed after the horse has mastered the haunches-in and out. This is basically the same demand on the horse but traveling on a diagonal line. Once you have the ability to bend your horse and have him move into that bend, you can begin working on half pass.

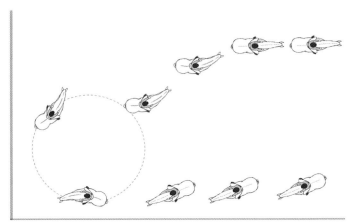

Introducing the half pass

One way to introduce the idea is by asking for a few steps early in the training when doing the walk exercise of leg yielding down the wall. Move into a circle with an outside bend. As you reach the centerline, ask the horse to move into the bend for a few steps of half pass before straightening him again.

If you have done the work in hand thoroughly, your horse will be able to move into the bend.

Beginning Half Pass

As most horses are more comfortable moving towards the rail, it is a good idea to begin your half pass by riding a small half circle at the end of one long side and asking for some steps of half pass back towards the track.

In the beginning work it is of vital importance that you remember the half pass is a forward movement. Do not try for too much sideways dis-

Moving the horse into the bend in half pass.

placement. Your inside leg must bend the horse and send him forward while the outside leg pushes gently to bring the outside hind across. The inside leg is more important than the outside leg.

In the early competitive tests, the angle of the half pass is quite gradual and you do not get too much crossing over. By the time you get to the Grand Prix level tests, the angle of the half passes is quite extreme and requires great strength and suppleness on the horse's part. Remember that you must develop the horse's strength and suppleness by degrees. In the early training of this movement if I find that my horse is beginning to struggle during a half pass, I will allow him to straighten and go straight ahead before I ask him again for the lateral movement. Alternating between a few good sideways steps and some energetic forward straight ones helps the horse keep his balance and impulsion.

All too often riders are so concerned about getting their horse to move sideways in the half pass that they concentrate on moving the horse from the outside leg and allow the hindquarters to lead the forehand.

The best way to avoid this is to start every half pass from a couple of steps of shoulder-fore. By positioning the horse for shoulder-fore, you ensure he is bent around your inside leg. You then change the dominant leg aid and ask the horse to move over from your outside leg. Riding a half pass after a corner using shoulder-fore for two or three steps gives you the correct bend and angle.

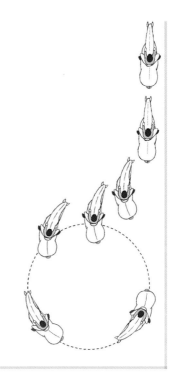

Half Pass from the Centerline and Half Pass to the Centerline

Once your horse can manage a half pass from the small half circle, you can ask for longer periods of lateral movement. Turn down the centerline and half pass back to the track. If you lose the bend at any point, straighten the horse, ride him forward a few steps, and ask again for the lateral movement. As your horse improves his ability to do this without losing his impulsion, you can ride from the track to the centerline.

Alternating Half Pass and Shoulder-In

When riding the half pass, you will find that your horse sometimes loses his bend. A good remedy when you feel the bend evaporating is to immediately ride your horse forward in shoulder-in.

You can alternate half pass and shoulder-in to maintain your horse's proper bend and impulsion. If you have been able to do the on and off the wall exercises successfully, this is simply another version using longer periods in each movement.

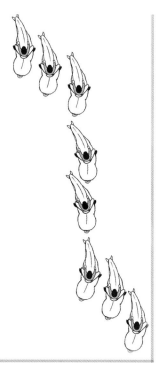

Alternating Half Pass and Shoulder-In

Moving from the shoulder-in to half pass.

Confirming the Half Pass

Nuno Oliveira often used an exercise he called "confirming the half pass." This exercise should be used once your horse can do a half pass from the centerline to the track. Ask him to continue down the track in *renvers* and, at the end of the track, ride a half-circle with the haunches still to the outside of the centerline. Restart your half pass to the opposite wall. When this exercise is ridden correctly, you will find that your horse has a better half pass the second time you ask.

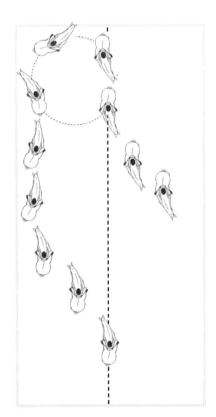

Counter Change of Hand

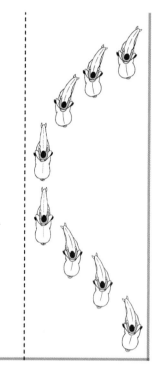

After you can ride the half pass successfully—to either direction, with good impulsion and swing—you can begin to change from one direction to the other. To teach the counter change of hand as this exercise is called, ask for a half pass out of the corner toward the centerline.

When first teaching this exercise, straighten your horse just before the centerline, ride several straight steps, ask for the opposite bend and return to the track. Eventually you will want to be able to ride this movement with only one straight stride between the two half passes.

In the beginning, however, it is easier on the horse to develop the movement in stages. If you ask for the first half pass away from the track, the horse will follow his natural tendency to return to the wall for the second one.

The difficulty of the movement is in riding the two half passes with the same angle, impulsion and suppleness. As all horses are one-sided, this is something you must keep in mind as you teach the exercise. As a judge, all too often I see the impulsion disappear as the horse hits his stiff side, and the bend in one half pass is much more distinct than the other. The aim of dressage is to make the horse equal on both sides—and that takes time.

The Zigzag

The zigzag is a series of counter changes performed from the center-line. As the horse progresses in his training, the dressage tests demand more and more complicated movements to demonstrate his suppleness and collection. In the zigzag, the important thing to remember is that each time you change the bend and move in a new direction, you run the risk of losing the impulsion, swing and bend. Only a well-muscled and responsive horse can perform this movement with ease.

In the beginning you need to keep your "zig" relatively small. Ride your first half pass about 5 meters from the centerline, and straighten the horse for a couple of steps before asking for the new bend and the new half pass. In this way you do not make a sudden change, but instead give the horse time to reorganize his weight and to move into the "zag."

Ride the second part of the movement, the "zag," five meters past the centerline, straighten, and ask for the original direction. In the beginning, it's likely you will not achieve four changes of direction as required in the tests. That doesn't matter. The important thing is that the horse remains calm and that he can shift his weight and bend while maintaining a trot that is full of energy.

Using Markers for Accuracy

Once you can make fluid changes of bend and direction, it's time to work on getting the geometry of the movement correct.

If you have trouble getting the zigs and zags even, try placing cones, surveyors' flags, or even buckets in your arena to show where each line finishes. A visual aid can be a super help for you to get the feel of this movement, which can be tricky as it takes place "out in space" in the tests, and not on the track at a convenient letter.

In the canter, the whole exercise is further complicated by having to include flying changes at each change of direction. This exercise is discussed in the chapter on canter.

6
Canter Exercises

The canter is perhaps the most important gait and the most difficult to refine. As you progress through the levels to the FEI tests, the canter work takes precedence. When choosing a horse for a dressage career, you must really consider the quality of the horse's canter. A horse with a good, reaching walk will nearly always have a good canter. A horse that has a fantastic trot but only a so-so walk and canter will be more difficult to train to the higher levels. The old truism is that while you can always improve the trot, a dressage horse must have three good gaits.

The canter is more difficult to improve as it is the odd gait out: it is an asymmetrical movement. The most important factor to consider when evaluating a horse's canter is the amount of natural suspension he shows while cantering. A canter with a longer period of suspension will be much easier to deal with when you come to flying changes and advanced work. An earthbound canter with little clarity of beat will be hard to improve enough for the work at the upper levels.

The hind leg must jump up underneath the rider's body.

The horse shows an uphill balance in the entry into the arena.

The horse is straight.

The hind legs are carrying the weight so that...

...the horse can come directly down to a square, engaged halt.

Canter Departs

From the beginning of the horse's training you must pay strict attention to canter departs because, later on, the canter depart becomes the flying change. Teach your horse from the very beginning to make a straight depart, neither falling in on his inside shoulder nor bringing his haunches to the inside. If you just bring your outside leg back for the canter aid, the horse will tend to bring his haunches in. Use your inside seat bone and the inside leg at the girth to counterbalance the outside leg behind the girth.

You must be strict about this from the beginning. It helps to use a slight shoulder-fore position before asking for a depart from the trot. For the very young horse, it is best to ask for the canter going into a corner at the end of a long side, or going towards the wall while on a circle

Once you are past the initial breaking in of your horse and have begun to be more formal in the horse's education, time spent honing the canter depart will pay off handsomely in your future training.

Canter Departs on the Circle in Trot

Ride a circle in trot, ask for a canter depart, ride the circle in the canter, come back to the trot for two or three steps and ask for the canter again. Your aim here is to develop seamless transitions with the horse holding his balance and rhythm.

As you ride the canter, it is important to give a little canter aid every stride. Your inside seat bone should swing forward and follow the movement of the saddle. Your outside leg stays a little behind the girth to keep the outside hind leg, the propelling leg, jumping up under the body. When you want to come back to trot, you have only to stop giving the canter aid with your body and bring your outside shoulder back in order to place more weight on the outside hind.

This action "grounds" the hind leg so that the horse begins to trot from behind and does not fall forward onto his forehand and rush. If you repeat this exercise several times, you will find that your horse, by anticipating the demands, becomes more and more able to balance himself on his hind leg. Staying on a circle helps to balance the horse in the canter; riding a straight line is more difficult. Let the circle help you do the work. Ride these transitions until they become effortless and your horse stays in the balance and rhythm of the gait without rushing.

Canter Depart from Walk

Once you have mastered the canter depart from the trot in both directions and can easily do several effortless transitions, your horse will be ready to depart out of the walk. This will not happen in a day! It might take weeks before you are ready to move on.

Horses can canter from the trot, the walk, a halt, a rein back, a turn on the haunches, and a canter, with the latter exercise being a flying change. It is not necessary for the horse to rush into canter.

Pay attention to the timing of your aids. Many problems can be avoided if you give the aid at the correct moment so the horse has no trouble in deciphering your demands. The walk is a gait of four separate beats with the legs moving in a broken diagonal sequence. Left front, right hind, right front, left hind, for example. Since a canter stride begins with the outside hind leg bearing all the horse's weight and pushing his mass forward, you must ask for the depart as the opposite front leg steps forward. If you want a left lead, it is the right hind that will propel the canter, so time your aid for when the left front goes forward. Your horse is then in a position to bring his right hind under his body and give you a correct canter depart. To the right, give the aid as the right front steps forward, to enable the left hind to act.

Canter Depart from a Shoulder-Out Circle in a Walk

I have had great success in teaching young horses the canter depart from the walk by riding a circle in shoulder-out and, when approaching the open side of the arena, asking for a canter depart on a circle in the other direction. If I do a circle to the right in shoulder-out position, I ask for a circle in canter left on the open side (A). If I do a circle to the left in shoulder-out position, I ask for the right lead canter (B).

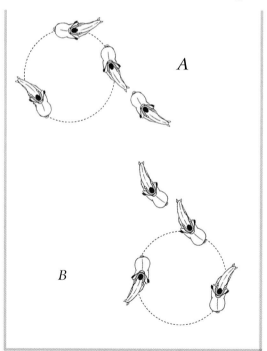

By pushing the hind legs under the body in the shoulder-out exercise, the horse is in a good position to make a balanced and smooth depart without resistance. The exercise has placed the horse just where he needs to be. Again it is the precise timing of the aids that make this work.

The canter of a horse in the early stages of training: forward but not a lot of engagement.

Using the Outside Rein Upward in the Depart

Some horses have great difficulty in the early stages of training in taking one lead or the other. You can help this type of horse by using your outside rein upward, toward the horse's ears at the moment of depart. By raising the outside rein you effectively encourage the horse to line up on that side and put his body in front of the pushing leg. Pulling the head to the inside with the inside rein only brings the horse onto the inside shoulder and compounds his difficulty in taking the lead.

Using a Ground Pole to Get the Correct Lead

Some horses might need even more dramatic remedies until they are able to get the "difficult" lead. It can be useful to place a ground pole on in the corner of the arena and ask for the canter depart over the pole, going into the corner.

Work on the Circle

As soon as your horse can give you the correct canter lead in both directions, you can begin to really work in the canter.

The circle is your best exercise. Using the same exercises you used in the trot, ask the horse to decrease the circle into the middle of the arena until he can manage a 10-meter circle, and increase the size of the circle again. You are beginning to teach leg yield in the canter. Do not stay for a long time on the small circle in the early stages as this can be hard on your horse's hocks.

Small Circles within the Circle

The next step is to ride a forward canter on the big circle and ask for a 10-meter circle within the big circle, just as you did in the trot work; again see the illustration on page 47. After a few tries, you will find that you can ask your horse to move out on the outside circle in a longer frame, and begin to collect him for the smaller circles. Once this becomes easy for the horse, you can add a stretch down on the large circle, rebalance and lift the horse for the small circle.

Medium Canter and "Canter on the Spot"

A more advanced exercise that can be developed only after you can manage the previous one is to ask for a medium canter on the big circle for eight to ten strides, bring the horse back and try to canter "on the spot" for three or four strides. Send the horse energetically forward as soon as you feel you are about to stall out and lose the canter.

This exercise is a good preparation for the collection you will need to have in order to be able to ride the canter pirouettes. You do not want to stay in either canter for a long distance; it is the frequent adjustments of the horse's stride and shape in quick succession that constitute the valuable muscle-building work.

A more advanced balance in the higher levels. Uphill balance.

Good balance and bending of the quarters in preparation for the pirouette.

The Simple Change: Canter to Walk to Canter

When you can depart easily into the canter from the walk in both directions, you should begin to ask for a direct transition from the canter to the walk. By this time your horse will be more balanced in the canter and able to perform this exercise.

Again, it is the timing of the aids that makes this transition possible. The canter has three beats, the footfall of each stride is as follows: the outside hind, the diagonal pair, then the leading foreleg. The moment of suspension comes after the leading leg hits the ground: there is a moment when all four feet are in the air.

It is during the suspension that the horse can rearrange his feet and change gaits or, eventually, do a flying change. You must time your aid for the new gait to coincide with the leading leg. Remember that you have that little lag in time between the giving of the aid and the response. If you are riding the canter, following with your inside seat bone, with your inside leg on the girth and the outside leg slightly behind, you should be giving a minute canter aid every stride. To change the gait, all you have to do is bring your outside shoulder back and sit on your outside seat bone. Bringing your shoulder back when the horse is on a good contact will give you enough extra feeling on the outside rein to signal the horse to slow down.

If you switch seat bones emphatically, you put all your weight over the horse's outside hind leg and grounding it so the horse cannot jump through for the next canter stride. To do a transition to the trot you need a relatively little aid. To come to the walk, you need to be more definite but the aids, and the timing of the aids, are the same. Your seat should be moving with the canter, but stop following the movement as your outside shoulder goes back and you close your fingers on the outside rein.

For the first few times you ride a simple change, let the horse walk five or six steps before asking for the canter depart on the other leg. Don't hurry the horse for the first transitions. Let him settle, and then ask for the depart. If your horse does get rattled, understand that from his point of view you just asked him to walk and now you are asking for canter right away. This might be too much for him at first. So walk for several more steps before you ask for the depart. You can gradually decrease the number of walk steps. Ideally, in a simple change, three or four steps of walk are enough. But do not be in a rush to get there at the expense of your horse's mind!

The Small Circle in Walk with a Turn on the Haunches to Canter on the Same Circle

To work on the horse's collection and lightness I have found this exercise useful to help the development of engagement and balance.

Begin on the long side and ride a 10-meter meter circle in an active medium walk. Upon returning to the track, ride a turn on the haunches so that you are now facing the opposite direction, change the bend, and immediately ask the horse to canter on the same circle.

The value of the exercise lies in keeping your horse on the same circle. In the beginning you can ride two or three 10-meter circles in the canter and, upon reaching the track, bring the horse back to the walk on the same circle. On reaching the track, ride a turn on the haunches in the opposite direction and canter one or two circles again, and repeat the exercise.

When you have practiced the exercise, take the concept a step further and eliminate the walk circle. Canter the 10-meter circle, walk, ride a turn on the haunches and canter the opposite way. This is a much more advanced exercise. Wait until you are doing the first version with great ease and with a light and responsive horse before you try it. A word of warning: do not to do this exercise every day. It puts quite a strain on the horse's joints and mind, so use the exercise with discretion; once or twice a week is enough.

More Advanced Canter Departs

There are a variety of exercises to refine your canter departs as you progress up the ladder towards the advanced work.

One is to ride up the centerline in the left lead canter, paying close attention to the horse's straightness: if you use a slight shoulder-fore position, you will have a straight center-line. Toward the end of the school, ride the horse to the halt. Ride a turn on the forehand from your left leg and as soon as you are aligned back on the centerline in the opposite direction, ask for a left canter down the line.

At the other end of the arena, bring the horse down to a walk for two or three steps, ride a turn on the haunches to the left, and depart again in left lead canter back down the centerline. I find this exercise really teaches the rider to use the inside leg to help the horse into the correct lead without deviating from the line. It is of tremendous value for preparing straight changes.

Once you can do this to the left, reverse the process and ride in right canter to the turn on the forehand from the right leg to right canter. Then ride a turn on the haunches right to the right lead canter.

Ride the turn of the forehand and ask for the canter back on the centerline.

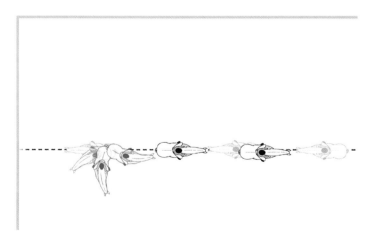

Ride the turn on the haunches and depart in the canter on the centerline.

Rein Back to Canter Depart

Another useful exercise to make your horse well balanced on his haunches in canter is to ride a canter depart from four or five steps of rein back. Here you ask for the rein back and, keeping your horse perfectly straight, ask for the canter depart from the last backward step. You can ride this on either rein and the quality of your canter in the first steps will be well-seated and collected.

It is difficult for the horse to make the depart directly from the rein back step. All his weight and momentum are going backward so he must step under himself to lift up and transfer the backward motion into a forward and upward canter step. The rein back must be fluid and resistance-free, coming mostly from leg pressure and not from pulling on the rein. You should lean slightly forward to rein back and bring your upper body back to vertical at the very moment you ask for the depart.

With your knowledge of the mechanics of the canter stride, you can determine which leg you want to be the leading leg and ask as the opposite diagonal pair of legs is stepping back. The left canter lead begins on the right hind and vice versa. If you time your aid for the depart precisely, the horse will have no trouble in giving you the required lead.

Walk Shoulder-In to Canter to Walk Shoulder-In

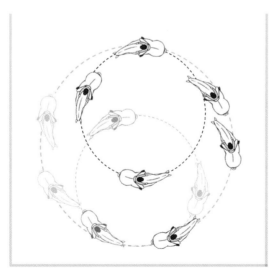

This exercise will help your horse engage in the canter.

On a large circle to the left at the walk, ride a shoulder-in. After a few steps, ask the horse for a left lead canter depart and ride a 10-meter circle inside the large circle. Upon the return to the large circle, ride a transition to walk with the first step going sideways in shoulder-in.

Allow the horse to settle into the shoulder-in and ask for another small canter circle, followed by another down transition, with the first step moving away from your inside leg. After a rest break, reverse and do the same exercise on the right rein.

Do not dwell on these exercises for any extended period. Remember to ride some medium and very forward long sides and diagonals in between these exercises to keep your horse thinking forward. It is a good idea to ride a large circle in canter and stretch the horse's neck down for an entire circuit in between these exercises. For example, practice the exercise to the left, go forward down the long side and ride a stretchy circle before asking for the exercise on the right rein.

Leg Yield in Canter

The leg yield ridden in canter is a great collecting and straightening exercise. You can ride it from the quarter line to the track and, later on, from the centerline to the track. Later still, it can be ridden from the track to the centerline.

In this exercise it is important to ask the horse to move from the inside leg to the outside rein. The outside leg must stay in contact to keep the canter stride and the outside rein must keep the neck straight. This brings the horse through from behind and rounds him over his topline.

Be careful not to use a strong inside rein as this tends to make the horse bend the neck only and avoid the gymnastic value of the exercise. Do not try to push the horse's shoulder over with the inside rein; this will only block the movement. You cannot ask the horse to move to the right from your left leg and ask him to stay to the left at the same time.

Later on, when the horse has learned to do changes, this is a good test of his obedience, to move from your inside leg without his changing lead. You must keep your inside leg forward in this exercise unlike in other leg yields when you bring the leg back a little.

Shoulder-In, Haunches-In, Haunches-Out

When the canter is balanced and has developed a degree of collection, you should ride brief periods of all the lateral movements to increase your horse's suppleness and engagement. Again, mix things up and ride these exercises in conjunction with some very forward movements. Ideally, you want to develop your horse's ability to contact the ground with his feet in a very clear rhythm and increase his ability to jump through with his hind legs well engaged. The beat of the canter should become more and more defined with a clear moment of suspension.

Alternating Shoulder-In and Haunches-In on the Circle

For this exercise, ride on a 20-meter circle and ask for a quarter circle in shoulder-in, reposition the horse, and ask for haunches-in on the next quarter circle. Repeat this on the second half of the circle.

On and Off the Wall in Canter

Bring the horse down the long side of the arena in the *entwickeln* exercises you used in the trot. Be especially careful with the placement of your legs in these exercises if the horse knows his changes. You must give crystal clear aids to prevent confusion on the part of the horse. By the time you can ride these exercises with good rhythm and relaxation, full of energy and impulsion, you are well on your way to be able to cope with the demands of the FEI tests.

The Canter Half Pass from a Small Half Circle

Once your horse can manage haunches-in on the circle in the canter, you can ask him for some shallow half passes. Begin with the left lead and, as you did in the trot work, ride a small half circle to the left, ask for the half pass back to the track, and continue down the track in counter canter.

Ride through the short end in counter canter and leg yield back toward the centerline and turn left. Change the rein, make a transition to the trot and pick up the right canter lead, riding the same exercise to the right.

Gradually increase the size of your small half circle until you can do a half pass from the centerline to the track. At this point, it is more important to keep the impulsion and jump of the canter than to do a steep half pass.

Half Pass from the Track to the Centerline and Straight Ahead

The next step is to ride from the long side to the centerline in a half pass. Canter on the left rein and prepare the horse coming out of the short side by riding a slight shoulder-fore position. Ask the horse to move toward the centerline. When you reach the centerline, canter straight ahead and turn left. Ride across the diagonal, change the lead (X) through the trot or by riding a simple change through the walk and repeat the exercise on the other rein.

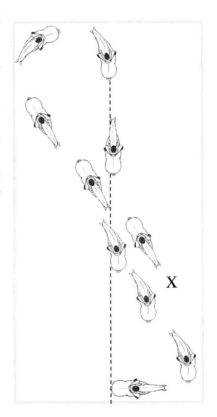

7

More Advanced Canter Work:
Counter Canter, Flying Changes & Pirouettes

Counter Canter

Once you have your horse in a good balance on both leads on circles and straight lines, it is time to think about using the counter canter to improve his straightness and suppleness.

Counter canter is a major suppling exercise and should be used throughout the horse's training. I find it invaluable in developing a good canter. Before I even consider teaching the flying change, I want my horses to be able to do extended periods of counter canter without any struggle whatsoever.

The counter canter, straight and balanced.

In the beginning, this is a tiring exercise for the horse as it increases the demand on his inside hind leg. It must not be overdone. Introduce short periods for the first month or so and gradually increase the amount of counter canter so that the horse grows in strength and you do not injure him. Always remember that the rhythm and impulsion must be maintained. If the horse breaks or cross canters, do not make a big deal about it. Just come down to the walk and restart the exercise. Above all, if your horse gives you a flying change at any point, do not scold him for doing so.

It is easier to introduce the counter canter in an open space. If you have a large area or even an open field, you are not as restricted in your choice of direction and the horse will not be as pressured.

Riding a Loop

Most horses are more relaxed in the left lead canter, although there are a few exceptions. If your horse is one of those exceptions, begin with the right lead. Otherwise begin with the left lead canter.

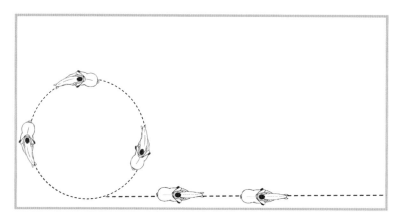

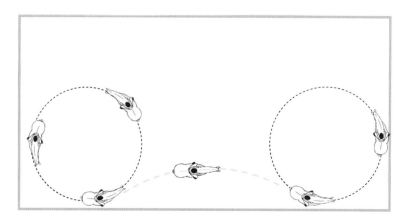

Canter a large circle to the left and ride forward in a straight line. Canter another circle to the left and this time, instead of riding a straight line, ride a loop, starting out by going to the left and gradually bringing the horse back to the right in the same canter. Make sure your horse stays slightly positioned to the left throughout the entire exercise.

If this exercise presents little problem to your horse, you can go on to the next. However, if your horse breaks, or changes, be patient, start over and make the the size of your loop more shallow.   If the horse has a good canter, this exercise should present no problem. Once you can do this to the left, change the rein and ask for the same exercise to the right.

Half Circle and Return to the Track

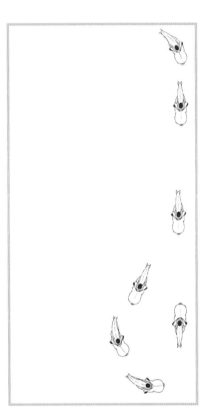

The next exercise is to ride a half circle and return to the straight line in the counter lead. If you are in a big space, this should present no problem. If you must do your work in an arena, ride back to the middle letter, E or B, and ride down the track in counter canter.

The first few times you would be wise to trot just before you reach the corner. But as soon as your horse is comfortable, you can ride around the end of the arena in counter canter to the next long side, and continue down that side. Do not try to take the horse deep into the corner and, in the beginning, do not try and ride across the diagonal at the end of the short side. You can do that later as the horse becomes more used to the counter canter. Be content with keeping the canter in rhythm and balance, giving the horse plenty of space in which to move. After all, you taught the horse to canter on the "correct" lead, and now you are introducing a new concept that contradicts that idea.

The Serpentine

The next stage is to ride a serpentine of three loops on the same lead. Begin with a loop in left lead canter followed by a loop to the right in left lead, and return to the left for the third loop. Your loops should be even. Do not cheat and make the true canter loops smaller than the counter canter one. I often see this as a judge when riders ride this movement in tests and it is avoiding the difficulty. The loops must be even and regular in size and the horse must be able to stay in exactly the same canter on either lead.

When your horse can hold the canter lead in these beginning exercises, you are ready to use the counter canter as a valuable training tool. It took me some years before I realized just how much benefit can be gained by riding counter canter to improve, straighten and supple the horse.

The Small Loop Serpentine

In this exercise you ride a shallow serpentine of five loops, about three meters to each side of the centerline. The value of this is the frequent changes of direction. Again, keep the forward feeling in your canter. If you are working in a large space, the serpentine can be extended for as many loops as you feel like riding. All these exercises help to make your horse adjustable and handy.

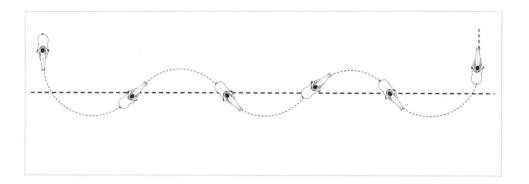

The Small Loop Serpentine

The Serpentine Including Small Circles

A more advanced serpentine exercise in to ride the first loop in true canter, ride a small circle on reaching the centerline, followed by the counter canter loop, and a small circle again in the true canter on reaching the centerline. Finish with the third loop in true canter.

Serpentine Beginning with Counter Canter

A much more advanced exercise would be to ride the serpentine starting out in counter canter with the middle loop ridden in true canter. This is much more difficult and should come only after you can do the first serpentine exercises easily.

Alternating Leg Yield and Half Pass

The leg yield in canter is helpful in increasing the collection as long as you keep your horse straight using the outside rein and do not allow a bend. Once you can ride both the leg yield and the half pass in canter, you can combine the two exercises.

Start from the corner in counter canter and ask the horse to leg yield toward the centerline. When you reach the centerline, reverse your leg aids and ask for a half pass towards the track again. You must be quite clear with your leg aids in this exercise and use your inside leg, the inside leg to the canter, quite far forward in the leg yield so that the horse does not try to change.

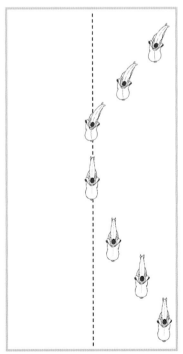

Alternating from leg yield to half pass on the right lead.

You can also ride this combination by riding a half pass toward the centerline, change over and leg yield back to the track again. The whole exercise is similar to the "on and off the wall" exercise you have ridden earlier, but with longer sections of each phase. This makes your horse responsive and teaches him to pay close attention to your legs.

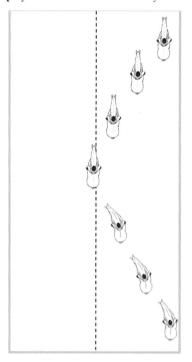

Alternating half pass to leg yield on the left lead.

Counter Canter in Counter Flexion

Before I even think of teaching the flying changes, I work a great deal of counter canter to prepare my horse for the next step. This exercise is great preparation.

Bring your horse a little off the track at the beginning of one long side and ask for the counter canter from trot or walk. Return to the track and counter canter around the next short end. Down the next long side, stay in counter canter, and ask the horse to bring his head and neck into the arena. You are asking the horse to counter flex. As you reach the next short side, return to the outside flexion, the flexion of the canter. Continue on, asking for a counter flexion on the long side and the correct flexion on the short ends.

Medium and Collected Counter Canter

For this exercise, ride medium canter down the long side in counter canter, and make a definite transition to a more collected canter to go through the short end.

Oliveira was a great believer in the counter canter but warned, "It must not be overdone, as then instead of having a beneficial effect, it will come to have a harmful one." So, heed the master: do not work on this day after day, but maybe once or twice a week.

Figure Eight's

As your horse develops balance and suppleness in the counter canter, you can go from riding the serpentine to riding a figure eight while maintaining the same canter lead. Ride a circle to the left on the left lead, followed by a circle to the right on the left lead, and return to a left lead canter circle. Repeat the exercise using the right lead for the first circle.

Flying Changes

A straight flying change.
Left: The horse is in the final step of right lead canter, the right fore hitting the ground.
Below left: The horse comes into the air perfectly straight: you can see right through the line of his legs.
Below: And down he comes on the left lead.

There are many different ways to introduce the flying change, but all of them require that the horse has been well prepared by work on the canter depart. Each horse is different and you may have to experiment to see which method makes sense for your horse. Much depends upon the temperament and athletic ability of the horse, but the work is always easier if you have taken the time to make the horse straight in his canter.

When do you teach the changes? The only answer is "When the horse is ready." That is something you must judge for yourself with every horse. A horse with a God-given canter can do his changes early on, while a horse that is stuck in his shoulders, or is very crooked in one canter or the other, will need to be worked diligently to correct those issues before you even attempt a change.

Oliveira's Method of Teaching the Changes

For the horse with a good canter, you might want to use Oliveira's method of teaching the change. For this, your horse should be able to do simple changes anywhere in the arena, even on a circle, changing from true canter to counter canter on a 20-meter circle promptly and without resistance.

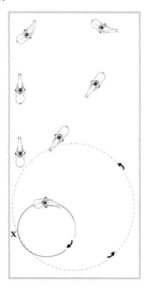

Stage 1

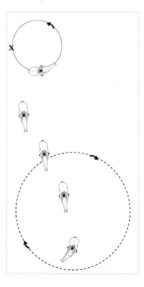

Stage 2

Stage 1

Ride a small volte in the right lead canter at the beginning of the long side, ride a simple change to the counter canter left lead (X), continue down the long side and around the short end. Change the rein and ride a 20-meter circle, with a volte at the beginning of the opposite long side, and do a simple change to the right lead canter. Continue down the long side, through the short end, and leg yield to the centerline and turn right. Ride a large circle with the horse's neck stretched down. Walk and let the horse relax.

You may want to spend a couple of weeks doing this. Gradually reduce the number of walk steps in the simple change until you can do the change with a single walk step, and the horse clearly understands that you want him to change the lead at the beginning of the long side.

It may well be that the horse offers you a change on his own, in which case you should praise him effusively. It will be apparent to you which change will be the easier one; that is the one you need to ask for on your first attempt at the flying change. For the majority of horses this will be the change from the right lead to the left lead. When it is easy to obtain the simple change with only a single walk step, you can ask for the flying change upon reaching the track after your volte. Since you have conditioned the horse to expect to change at this point he should be able to give you a true change. Do not give a strong aid for the change. If the horse is responsive, it is better to use a light, precise aid rather than excite the horse by using harsh aids.

Asking the horse to change against the wall of the arena keeps him from swinging his haunches in, and you can achieve straight changes from the very beginning of your work.

Stage 2

Once your horse can manage the first stage, you can progress to riding a leg yield away from the track after you do your simple change to the counter canter. Upon reaching the end of the arena turn back to correct canter and ride a large circle.

Stage 3

Now ask the horse for the flying change after the small circles (F) and stay in the counter canter down the long side and through the short end and change the rein again.

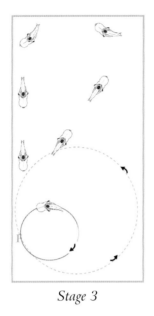

Stage 3

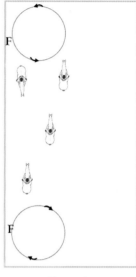

Stage 4

Stage 4

This is an advanced exercise. Once your flying changes are confirmed, ride the change out of the volte and immediately leg yield to the center-line. At the end of the arena, turn in the correct canter and ride another volte at the beginning of the long side. Ride a flying change and leg yield to the center again.

Change from a Half Circle and Return to the Track

Another exercise for beginning flying changes is to ride a half circle to the centerline at the end of the long side and return to the track at the middle letter. Once you are straight on the track, ask for a simple change from counter canter to true canter. Again, in setting the horse up progressively by reducing the number of strides in the walk, you show him that a change of lead is coming at a certain place on the wall.

Change from a Half Circle and Half Pass

For horses that need more engagement of the hind leg, it is useful to ride a half circle and return to the track in a half pass. Ask for the change from the counter canter as you straighten on the wall.

Change in the Corner

For horses that are weaker in their quarters, it helps to ask for the change at the end of a long side. Ride down the long side in a forward counter canter, collect the horse at the end as practiced in the counter canter work, and ask for the change going into the corner.

This method has the disadvantage of allowing the horse to become crooked for the change, but horses with weaker canters find this method easier as they find relief from the demands of the counter canter.

I once had a thoroughbred that was quite weak behind and I spent an entire clinic under the direction of Oliveira trying to get a change. We spent four days flying around the arena at top speed attempting the changes and being totally unsuccessful. On the fourth day, I was using a strong change of bend in the corner and went home thinking to myself "I think he's got it." The next day we came in and the horse changed leads upon demand. He went on to do the easiest changes of any horse I have ever ridden.

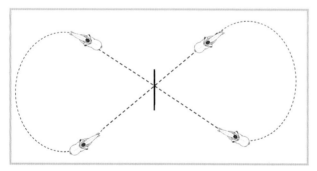

Introducing the flying change using a rail in the center of the arena.

For difficult cases, place a cavalletti or small jump in the middle of the arena and ride the horse at an angle to the jump on one lead. Ask for the change to the other lead as the horse jumps the rail.

Some trainers advocate teaching the changes from one circle to the other. This can lead to difficulty with the straightness; I believe in practicing straight changes from the very beginning. It is easier to teach straightness from the very beginning, rather than having to "fix" crookedness later.

Changes Closer Together

When the horse has accepted the flying changes on both sides, you can begin to work toward asking for more frequent changes closer together. Do not be in a hurry with this work. Remember to build the skills carefully so the horse has time to accept each new demand. Teaching the changes should never be hurried so that the horse is never forced or rushed.

Once you can do the change to the counter canter after the volte at the beginning of the long side in the exercise above, and your horse accepts this readily, begin the leg yield to the centerline after the change and turn back into the true canter at the end. Ride the other volte right away and ask for the second change.

Another useful exercise is to ride the change to the counter canter at the beginning of the long side, ride a change to true canter in the middle of the side, and ride a third change at the end back into counter canter. Once you can achieve three changes on the long side, you are probably ready to try the tempi changes. If you concentrate on getting easy, fluent changes in the beginning work without worrying about the number of strides, you will not pressure the horse unduly at this stage.

When your changes are established on both reins, you can begin to insist on definite striding between changes. I find that by asking for changes every six and then every five strides in the beginning, I do not upset my horse by demanding changes closer together. That will come once the horse is obedient and relaxed.

Once you begin the work on changes, horses tend to anticipate. You must do a great deal of counter canter and straightforward canter work interspersed with the work on changes. Horses get upset if drilled too often on these exercises.

Do not always ride your tempi changes on the diagonal: you must be able to ride a change at any point in the arena. If you do changes only on the diagonal, it will come back and haunt you in the future if you have to ask for a change elsewhere in the arena.

If your horse tends to be crooked on one side, ride that change against the wall. If your horse swings his hindquarters to the right, ride on the left lead down the track and do the change to the right, towards the wall. If your horse is crooked to the left you want to ride on the right lead and do the left change towards the wall.

Remember to ride the changes forward in a slightly more energetic canter. All too often I see horses doing the required number of changes in a test, but each successive change gets shorter and shorter. Good changes stay forward and jump through with energy and cover the ground. With a horse that does good changes you should barely be able to fit in the required number across the diagonal.

Once you have taught the horse to do the changes every two strides and the horse is comfortable with the idea, you can begin the changes every stride. It is better to teach the changes every stride on the short side since the horse is used to being collected through the short end.

Begin by asking for two consecutive changes. Do the more difficult change first and immediately reverse your aids and ask for the easier one. As you ride into the short end in true canter, straighten the horse, half halt, and give the aid for a change to the counter canter. Immediately reverse your aids and ask for the true canter again. If you succeed the first time you ask, come back to the walk, praise the horse, and repeat the exercise on the next short end.

Once you can ride two one-time changes on the short end, try the same exercise on the diagonal. The most important things to remember are to keep the horse calm, forward, and straight. The one tempi changes come so close together you do not have time to do any major changes in the position of the horse's head and neck. In fact, if you try to change the bend too much, you create changes that swing off the line. Good one-time changes go forward with impulsion and absolutely straight. Each horse is a little different, but I find that the more I can do with my seat bone, the less I do with my hand, and the quieter I keep my legs, the easier the exercise becomes for the horse.

When you can manage the two changes, add a third one. Here it is better to ask for the easier change first, followed by the more difficult one, and back to the easy one. Once you can get three changes, adding more becomes progressively easy. The rhythm takes over, and you and your horse get into the swing of the movement. I find that the two-time and one-time changes are actually much easier to ride than the four-time changes. I do not seem to be able to count to four.

Whenever you do ride a series of one-time changes, it is wise to ride a set of two-times afterward, and to finish the session with counter canter around the arena. Horses are so smart they will need to be reminded that they are only to change when you ask.

Variations of the Serpentine

Some horses, once they learn the changes, are delighted to offer you a change any time you change direction. They must be persuaded that this is not correct and that they must wait for you to ask for the change.

Serpentines are a good exercise to improve both suppleness and obedience. Ride a three loop serpentine with no changes and then ride another one asking for a change each time you cross the centerline.

Next, increase the number of loops and ride a four loop serpentine with no changes and then one with a change on the first and third loop with counter canter in between.

The old FEI Intermediare 1 test included a six loop serpentine, with the first and second loop in true canter, the third and fourth in counter canter, with a change from counter canter to counter canter in the middle at X, and the last two loops in true canter.

In other words, you ride the first loop and do a change on the centerline to the second loop, then ride a counter canter loop with no change. Ride a change at X from counter canter to another counter canter loop, the next loop in true canter, and change again for the final loop. This is a true test of your horse's ability to remain on the aids throughout the entire exercise.

Counter Change of Hand

Teaching the counter change of hand should not be a problem if the horse is established in the changes. The first step is to ride the half pass towards the centerline, ride a flying change and go straight on. You can also ride the half pass from the centerline to the track and ask for the change there.

The next step is to put both these concepts together. In the beginning, it is best to ride four or five straight strides on the centerline before asking for the change and the second half pass. If you take the time to get a straight change on the centerline, you will find this exercise is not so difficult. The most difficult part is getting the half passes even in both directions. Here again you might put some cones or markers in your arena to help you work out the geometry of the movement.

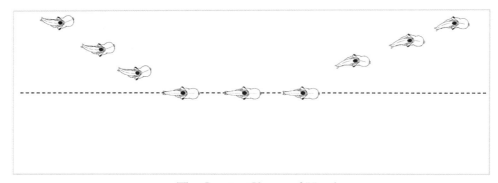

The Counter Change of Hand

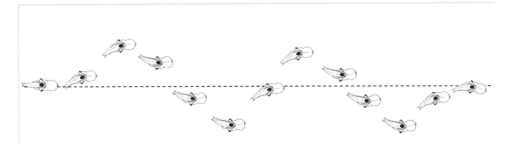

The Zig Zag in Canter

The Zigzag in Canter

There is a video of the British Olympian Jenny Loriston-Clarke riding a free style test where she executes a flawless zigzag in canter-riding with one hand. As I have sometimes struggled with the zigzag, I am always overcome with admiration each time I watch this.

This exercise is not asked for in a dressage test until you reach the Intermediare tests. The first time it is asked for, you are asked to ride the movement five meters to each side of the centerline and only three half passes are required; the number of strides is not specified. In Intermediare 2, however, you must ride a specific number of strides in between the changes, and ride four half passes, which immediately makes them steeper. The movement is four strides, change, eight strides, change, eight strides, change, four strides and straight on.

Three Half Passes

It is useful to have markers in your arena when riding this exercise. There is much to think about: the quality of the canter jump, the impulsion, the flying change and change of bend to the new half pass, as well as the geometry of the movement in the arena. It takes practice to get it right.

Break the movement up into its segments and make sure you know exactly how far you are to ride to the side of the centerline. As the first test asks for 5 meters from the centerline, you will reach the quarter line before you straighten and ask for the change to the new lead. Next you ride to the opposite quarter line to make the second change, and back to the centerline with a change on the centerline before you turn. You will have three half passes and three flying changes in this movement.

In your counter changes the angle of the half pass is relatively gradual, but now you are asking for a steeper angle. Prepare for this by riding half pass from the centerline to the quarter line, riding a change and moving straight on. This is an exercise that you must not rush to perfect. There is so much going on that the horse needs time to understand. Do not worry about counting strides: concentrate on getting an even canter and a smooth change. Above all, you must be able to ride equal half passes. Most horses go more easily to one side than the other; you must work on the difficult side to make him equal on both sides so you wind up in the correct place in the arena.

This is not an exercise to practice daily. Instead, give the horse a lot of work on perfecting the canter in balance, and work on the quality of both your collected and extended canters.

Four Half Passes with Required Number of Strides

The increased difficulty of this exercise often makes the rider get over anxious to achieve the correct number of strides. Only when you are able to ride the easier zigzag without being too rigid about the strides, and your horse is willing to do a flying change and change the direction without losing rhythm or getting overly excited, can you begin to think about being more precise.

Here again it is the quality of the canter and the relaxation of the horse that makes this more complicated exercise possible. To begin, divide this exercise into two parts. Ride the first half pass of four strides, ride a change, ride the second half pass of eight strides, ride a change and ride straight down the quarter line. Repeat the exercise by starting at the quarter line, riding the eight strides to the opposite quarter line, and doing a change, coming back to the centerline. In this manner you show your horse the exercise without demanding too much.

Next, ride three of the required half passes, finishing on the second quarter line, and ride straight and forward. When you can successfully do this much, it is relatively easy to add the final short half pass at the end of the movement. In this way you build the horse's ability and confidence instead of asking for the whole exercise at once.

Any time the horse becomes too excited or resistant, ride him straight and forward and do some relaxing movement such as stretching down on a circle. The calmer you can keep your horse, the quicker he will learn the new demands.

The horse needs exceptional strength and balance to do a good pirouette.

In this photo the horse is not as "seated" and the exercise will not be as easy.

Pirouettes

The canter pirouette is one of the most difficult of all dressage movements. Both horse and rider must be in perfect balance and the horse must have a great deal of power and muscle to be able to perform it successfully. It is a true test of good training. Nowadays in the musical freestyles, we see double pirouettes as a norm.

The Spiral on the Circle

You can introduce the idea of the pirouette by using your spiral on the circle. To prepare your horse for the actual exercise, spiral in gradually with the horse in a slight shoulder-in position until you reach a small circle. As soon as you feel your horse is losing the canter beat, enlarge your circle and refresh your canter jump.

The Circle with Half Pirouettes in the Walk

This is a good exercise to prepare the horse for work on pirouettes as well as to improve the balance in the canter at any time in the training at this level. Ride a 20-meter circle in the canter, make a transition to walk for one or two steps, ride a half pirouette in walk, change the bend, and ask a canter depart in the new direction. Repeat this several times on the circle, cantering halfway around the circle, and asking for the turn and the canter in the new direction.

Canter Square

Remember riding the square at the walk in the beginning of your training? You can use the same idea to develop the pirouette. Bring your horse into the middle of the arena; it is easier to be in an open space than to be against the wall.

Canter a circle and begin to collect your horse as you do when you ride the medium canter followed by the canter on the spot. Ask the horse to collect and, at the same time, bring his forehand around with your outside rein and ask for a quarter turn. As soon as you have accomplished two steps ride straight forward. Collect and ride another quarter turn of two steps. Continue on to make four turns on your square. It is important to keep the jump of the canter and to be able to ride straight forward after asking for two steps of the turn.

Ride quarter pirouttes on a square in the canter.

Note that many of the difficulties in riding the pirouette are caused by the rider using too much inside rein to turn the horse. Sit in the middle of your horse and turn your head to the inside, keeping your inside leg on the girth to keep the bend and activity of the horse's inside hind leg. Bring your outside leg a little back from the girth to bring the horse's outside hind leg under the body. You should then be able to bring the shoulders around with the outside rein, just as you did when riding the square in the walk. The concept is the same. The most important fact to remember in the beginning is to keep the canter active. By asking for only two steps on the spot, you have a better chance of keeping your canter active.

Once you can ride this exercise in both directions, asking for only two steps on the spot, begin to ask the horse to make three steps and ride forward. Eventually you will want to ride four steps in the half pirouette. A full pirouette takes six to eight steps of canter to be correctly performed. In the half pirouette you need only to achieve four steps and be able to ride straight forward out of it. Often riders worry so much about the half pirouette, they forget that they have to ride out of it on a straight line, but this is all part of the exercise.

The Pirouette from a Half Pass toward the Wall

Begin this exercise on the lead that is most comfortable for your horse.

Ride a half pass from the centerline toward the wall. Just past the quarter line, straighten and ride a small volte toward the wall, and continue your canter half pass back to the other side of the arena. You can repeat the exercise on the other side of the arena. The wall will help you make a very small turn, and you can decrease the size of your turn even more as your horse understands the exercise.

Counter Canter to Half Pirouette and Three-Quarter Pirouette toward the Corner

Another valuable lesson to teach the horse is to ride in counter canter down the long side, about five meters off the track, on the horse's easier side. Ask for the half pirouette into the corner at the end of the long side.

Here you must ride the horse straight into the turn and straight again after the turn. By turning into the corner, the wall effectively holds the horse for you, and you only have to concentrate on keeping the canter jump active for four strides and not letting the horse stall out.

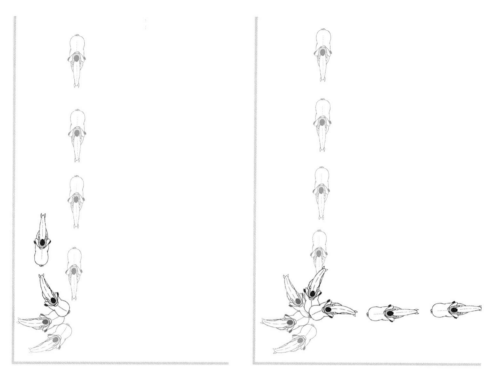

Counter Canter to Half Pirouette   *Counter Canter to Three-Quarter Pirouette*

After you have worked on this exercise successfully for the half pirouettes on both reins, you can go on to ride a three-quarter pirouette using the same method. This time you will do about six steps and continue on along the short end of the arena.

Problems in the pirouettes arise when the collected canter is not energetic and balanced. If you have problems in the execution of the pirouette, return to the work of developing a good collected canter using the lateral movements and frequent changes between medium and collected canter on the circle. If you do not have sufficient energy, the horse will drop out of the canter, try to spin around, try to change legs behind, or resist. When that happens, the horse is only trying to tell you that he cannot do the pirouette in a poor canter.

In the early stages be content with small circles performed in a good rhythm and balance and only reduce the size of the pirouette as the horse gains sufficient strength and collection. Keep in mind you are collecting energy.

Once you can ride good half and three-quarter pirouettes, it is only a matter of time before you can ask for the full pirouette. Remember that it is the ability to keep the quality of the canter and the rhythm that makes truly good pirouettes possible.

Walk Pirouette to Canter Pirouette

In the early days of musical freestyle competition, riders came up with the idea of doing a walk pirouette directly into the canter pirouette. Since then this has been not scored as a canter pirouette. The rules now require some steps of canter on a straight line before the pirouette. The walk pirouette to canter pirouette is not an easy exercise to pull off, but it can be of use to both you and the horse.

Ride a complete pirouette in walk, a 360 degree turn, ask for the canter depart, and continue on around in a canter pirouette. There must be excellent collection and excellent impulsion to perform this movement, and it is best left until your horse is well established in his canter pirouettes.

8

Exercises for Improving
Strength and Balance

With all the work you must do to advance your horse in his development, bear in mind that the horse is an animal and must have variety in his routine. Your regular routine should include work outside in the open, both for your horse's mental state and his physical strength. A horse was not created to spend his life in a 20 by 60 meter arena enclosed by a white fence. Going up and down hills helps to balance the horse and build his strength. You should spend time in all three gaits on hills until the horse can maintain the same speed and rhythm, neither rushing up the slope nor running down on his forehand.

Using Hill Work

An excellent exercise is trotting uphill with the horse stretched down. This makes him use his hind leg to push and so is useful in developing the lengthening in trot. After riding up the hill, turn and ride downhill, keeping the horse very straight to work on his collection. It is vital that you keep your horse completely straight because that requires him to bend the joints of the hind legs in order to cope with the terrain. Alternate these two exercises and you will find your horse reaching out to ascend the hill and engaging his hind leg in the descent.

Work over Cavalletti and Poles

Allow the horse to trot beside the poles to relax him before going over them.

From the beginning of your training, use cavalletti to encourage the horse to take even and regular strides. You can ask for longer or shorter strides by using the poles set on a curve with the inside ends four feet apart and the outside ends six feet apart.

I always teach the horse to do this on the lunge first and then ride over the same formations.

Begin this exercise with the cavalletti or poles set flat on the ground and progress to setting them higher to increase the suspension between the horse's steps. This must be done gradually so that the horse builds his strength and does not get upset.

You can also use poles to regulate your canter strides. At first, use spacing of 18 to 20 feet between the poles. Later on you can reduce the spacing by increments of one foot for shorter strides, or increase the spacing to lengthen the strides.

Exercises for Teaching the Horse to Lengthen and Extend the Trot

Some horses have great difficulty in learning to lengthen easily. While horses that have naturally big trots find it easy to obtain a good lengthening, others must be helped along to achieve this. The following exercises can help your horse understand.

The horse is trotting through the poles close to the edge in the shorter distance. Note the increased lifting of the legs.

On the Lunge Line

You can use you lunging session to teach your horse to lengthen. Bring him in close to you at the beginning of the long side and put him on a small circle. As he approaches the wall, stay just behind his shoulder and begin to run in a straight line parallel to the track, taking as long a step as you can manage. The horse will pick up on your rhythm.

At first it is difficult to time your move correctly; this exercise requires good coordination on your part. Essentially you want to trap the horse against the wall and drive him straight forward after the small circle. Many horses will canter as soon as you start to run, in which case just bring the horse back to the small circle and start over. As soon as the horse breaks, stop moving and patiently bring him back to the small trot circle. If you get ahead of the horse, he may have the opposite reaction and actually stop. Do not get ahead of the horse as then you lose your driving power.

This exercise can be ridden out in the open on a slight slope uphill, but you need to be fit yourself to be able to keep up!

Work Beside Another Horse

I have had success with some horses by riding them alongside a horse that already has a good lengthening. If you ride side by side across the diagonal, for instance, and keep your horse close to the other one, he will often pick up on the rhythm to keep up and offer a lengthening himself. The effect is akin to carriage horses that pick up on the rhythm of their harness mate.

Shoulder-In to Lengthening

You can use a short period of shoulder-in to engage the horse's inside hind leg, and then ask the horse to lengthen across half the diagonal. It is best to ask for a few longer steps and to repeat the exercise, rather than to try for too many and end up with a hurried rushed trot. It requires a lot of strength on the horse's part to have a good lengthening and, eventually, the extensions, and you must give the muscles time to develop.

Haunches-In and Medium Trot on a Circle

Once the horse has developed a medium trot out of the lengthening, work on building his engagement by using short periods of lateral work and asking for a few steps of medium trot.

Bring the horse onto a 20-meter circle and ride haunches-in with a pronounced bend to the inside. Ride about a quarter of the circle, straighten the horse, and go immediately into a medium trot for the next quarter circle. Recollect and ride haunches-in again. This is strenuous work for your horse so you do not want to do too much of it. Ridden judiciously, this exercise can help develop the medium trot because of the engagement you achieve with the haunches-in.

All too often you see riders trying to work their medium and extended trots over the entire diagonal, and the horse not able to maintain the energy for that long a period in the early stages of his training. Be content with short bursts of power, reestablish your engagement and go again. Any time you ride a medium or extended trot in a test, you want to ask for power at the beginning and then ask again for more power as you reach X to prevent the loss of impulsion.

In the medium and extended trot the cannon bones of the front and hind legs should remain parallel. You can see here that the horse has dropped his back a little and is flipping his front feet. The hind leg also lacks engagement.

A much better trot, well engaged and parallel.

9

Piaffe and Passage

The piaffe and passage are the ultimate development of trot work. With most horses it is wise to teach the piaffe first. Some horses have an extravagant elevated trot and find the passage easy to learn. The problem is that it is then quite difficult to get them to sit and piaffe on the spot as they enjoy showing off the passage.

Piaffe

I usually start work on the piaffe in hand, even with young horses, to give them the idea. It takes time and patience to develop a good piaffe; plan on a period of a year or more. The horse that has been introduced to the idea of piaffe early on in the work will show less resistance. The movement requires a great deal of muscle strength and you can only build muscles slowly and with much repetition.

Stand at the horse's shoulder and tap the croup. Here the trainer is a little too far forward.

Once the horse has learned the exercises in hand including the rein back, you can think about developing a few steps of piaffe. Ask for a rein back and some steps forward, then another rein back. This places the horse's haunches well under the body. Tap the horse on top of the croup and see if he will lower his haunches and take one or two steps with the hind legs. You can allow the horse to advance slightly but must hold the short rein on the cavesson to prevent the horse from merely walking forward.

The horse will have no idea what you want and you must reward the slightest attempt at moving the hind feet under the body. Lots of praise and even treats are powerful persuaders so that the horse begins to anticipate the reward. At first it is best to let the horse advance very slightly forward to help the horse understand. Often the horse will kick out, buck, or try to shoot past you. Be patient and persistent.

In the beginning it sometimes it helps to have an assistant help you. Your assistant holds the front end and you work on the haunches without having to hang onto the rein.

I had one horse that we never were able to hold in place and I gave up after he walked right over the top of my assistant. I had to resort to teaching him the piaffe from the saddle, but this is rare; most horses can be started in piaffe from the ground.

In addition to the whip you can also use your voice to good effect. Develop a good "click" which you can carry over to the mounted work. Basically, you are setting up a conditioned reflex so ask in the same way every time. Horses learn better from consistency.

This is a typical reaction in the early stages. The horse does not understand and is objecting. Remain calm and keep tapping gently. If this was a young Lippizan, he would be noted as a prospect for working the Courbette!

The same horse has now settled down and is beginning to bend his haunches properly. Note that this photo was taken only moments after the one at left.

By allowing the horse to advance slightly, you begin to get the diagonal legs lifting together.

The horse is bending and lifting the hind leg.

Once the horse has the concept of trotting in place with well-lowered quarters you can move on to working from the saddle.

The classical work is to ask for three or four short steps out of walk, then walk and repeat the question. You can help the horse understand by tapping with your whip on top of the croup behind the saddle. The most important thing to remember is that the horse must not be confused or pressed too hard in the beginning stages.

Take the time to develop the piaffe slowly and the horse will come to enjoy the work in a relaxed manner. Piaffe requires great strength and you build up muscles by asking for a little at a time with many repetitions. Work for short periods, reward the slightest indication of the correct response, and go do some other work in between. Do not try and insist on perfection in the early stages, and do not belabor the point.

The beginnings of real piaffe, lifting the diagonal pair of legs.

Passage

The horse that has lots of natural suspension and elevation in the trot will likely find the passage easy. Horses with less elevation must be carefully developed so they build up their strength before being asked to passage.

Bring the horse forward in hand once he has learned to piaffe by allowing him to move forward after several steps of piaffe. By using the whip on the front fetlock instead of on the croup you can usually get the horse to take the beginning steps of passage. Again, this is an exercise that must be approached carefully and by experienced trainers.

Using Cavalletti to Develop the Muscles and Raised Action of the Legs

When your horse has been lunged over cavalletti set at a normal spacing and is used to the concept, you can begin the work on passage. You need real cavalletti for this work, not just poles on the ground. Traditional cavalletti should be constructed so that you can roll them over and use three different heights.

Begin with the lowest setting and place the cavalletti just four feet apart on the inside of the curve. Once the horse can negotiate these, raise the setting to the second height. In the early training, I find it is best to keep the entry pole at the lowest height to get the horse into the exercise.

Begin with the cavalletti on the lowest setting and place them no more than four feet apart on the inside of the curve.

Once the horse can go in both directions over the lower setting, turn three of the cavalletti over to the second height. Leave the entry cavalletti at the lowest setting. Note the increased lifting of the legs.

Allow the horse to get used to this increased demand. Also, remember to reverse the exercise so the horse goes over the gymnastic on the right rein.

Raise three of the cavalletti to the highest setting and watch the effect on your horse.

Also, when I work on passage I do not use more than four cavalletti in a row. I do not want to put too much strain on the joints in these early stages.

Ask the horse to go through the gymnastic several times, then back away and let him canter forward on a circle as a break. Be sure to work the horse in both directions for an equal time. You want to develop symmetrical muscles. I work on this maybe two times a week and no more. By the time you are at this stage of training there is so much to work on, you need to choose your work carefully and mix it up. Do not drill on one exercise for too long a time.

Once the horse is able to trot through at the second setting easily without rushing or losing balance, put the cavelletti up to the highest setting and let the horse work with well-raised legs.

It may take a month of work to get to this next point, where you begin to ride the horse over the same settings.

Once again, start at the lowest setting and work up to the final height. Ride the horse through in a collected trot and encourage the swing of the back over the rails. Try to maintain the same feeling for several steps on the far side.

This horse is building all the requisite muscles for a lofty passage. Note the action of the hind leg as well as the forearm.

Alternating Extensions and Passage

Once your horse has the basic concept of passage, a valuable exercise is to practice passage alternating with the extended trot. I remember when this exercise was first introduced into the FEI tests. There were many who thought the demands would be too difficult. Strangely enough, however, it was found that this was of tremendous benefit to both the passage and the extension and the exercise has been included in the Grand Prix Special ever since. Passage requires a tremendous amount of impulsion, and alternating these exercises really develops the horse's strength and agility.

Final Words

In this book, I have shared a great many exercises I have found useful over the years. The problem with writing a book of exercises is that you could go on forever. There are countless exercises and we learn new and valuable combinations of work with every horse.

I can only hope that this book will give you some ideas for working on various problems with your horse. One of the joys of training horses is that it is a fascinating lifetime learning experience. I know it is for me.

Index